D1371044

"I've recently 'discovered' you and to my delight there was an intelligent cooking show, with food info presented by real chefs who obviously love what they are doing."

—Sybilla
Dartmouth, Nova Scotia

"You seem to have taken all the 'best' from other shows and wrapped it up into your 30 minute sensation. Congratulations."

—Faith
Cambridge, Ontario

"Easy, everyday cooking with great recipes. Keep up the good work."

—Kaye
Sudbury, Ontario

'It's so nice to watch you make good, healthy, low-fat recipes that can be whipped up in 30 minutes."

—Nancy
Surrey, British Columbia

"We love you both-you're the ying and yang of cooking."

—Joseph and Leo
Toronto, Ontario

"The two of you work so well together and make cooking so easy, quick and fun."

—Les
Winnipeg, Manitoba

BEST OF

What's for Dinner?

Recipes and Tattletales from Five Seasons

Ken Kostick

Prentice
Hall
Canada

A Pearson Company
Toronto

Canadian Cataloguing in Publication Data

Kostick, Ken, 1954-
    Best of What's for dinner?: recipes and tattletales from five seasons

Includes index.

ISBN 0-13-089849-X

1. Quick and easy cookery. 2. Cookery. I. Title.

TX833.5.K67 2000   641.5'55   C00-931464-4

ISBN 0-13-089849-X

Editorial Director, Trade Division: Andrea Crozier
Acquisitions Editor: Nicole de Montbrun
Copy Editor: Kat Motosune
Production Editor: Jodi Lewchuk
Art Direction: Mary Opper
Cover Design and Interior Design: Sharon Foster
Interior photos: courtesy Ken Kostick and Breakthrough Films and Television
Production Manager: Kathrine Pummell
Page Layout: Gail Ferreira-Ng-A-Kien

1 2 3 4 5 KR 04 03 02 01 00

Printed and bound in Canada.

Visit the Prentice Hall Canada Web site! Send us your comments, browse our catalogues, and more. www.phcanada.com.

A Pearson Company
Toronto

I want to dedicate this book to all the talented people who worked on *What's for Dinner* over five seasons. That list of names includes the entire staff of the television show, the production company and Life Network.

All of you truly made the show a wonderful success, and—just as importantly—you all made it fun. Thank you.

"Thanks for your enjoyable and friendly cooking show. I'll keep cheering
you in front of my TV every day!"

—Ryoko

Vancouver, British Columbia

"We find you show an inspiration."

—Frankie

Edmonton, Alberta

"My family and I have changed our bad eating habits to good and
healthy ones thanks to you both."

—Helen

Welland, Ontario

"I must confess that I am hooked, lined and sinkered."

—Neville

Toronto, Ontario

"I love your show, I love your show, I love your show…"

—Jackie

Port Moodie, British Columbia

"You guys are great and Ken is absolutely a doll. I love that you use so
many fresh vegetables and herbs."

—Patricia

Mississauga, Ontario

"The two of you working together make music for my dinner table."

—Shirley

Burlington, Ontario

Contents

"You two are a just a hoot together!"

—DOROTHY AND RAY

SARDIS, BRITISH COLUMBIA

"You make the kitchen fun."

—MIKE

NORTH BAY, ONTARIO

"Your recipes are so easy to follow, healthy and taste great."

—CAROL

NORTH VANCOUVER, BRITISH COLUMBIA

"Your recipes are mouth-watering, easy to follow and, most importantly, healthy."

—CHARLENE

LA PRAIRIE, QUEBEC

"...such simple recipes presented by you two become masterpieces!"

—MONIQUE

OTTAWA, ONTARIO

"My name is Hannah. I am eight. Me and my mom really, really like your show. I think it's the best!"

—HANNAH

SURREY, BRITISH COLUMBIA

"Enjoy your show very much. Even at 83 years old we can still learn a few tricks and lovely new recipes."

—ANN

ORILLIA, ONTARIO

Acknowledgments

I would like to acknowledge and thank certain people and organizations who helped make the *What's for Dinner?* television show and my follow-up cookbooks a resounding success:

Mary Jo Eustace—the best partner on television
Life Network/Alliance Atlantis: Barb Williams, Jim Ericson, Eleanor James and Sue Bowen
Breakthrough Films: Ira Levy and Peter Williamson
Dennis Saunders—the director
Lorrie Carstens—the assistant director
Amy Wilson—set design/props
Joanna Weinstein—the food stylist
Chris Duckett—food preparation
Jordana Ross—production
The Camera Crew
The Production Staff
The Researchers
The Kitchen Staff
Nicole de Montbrun—my cookbook editor
Celebrity Events/Daytime Enterprises: Lilana, Lorie, Kathy and Marion
Prentice Hall Canada/Pearson Education Canada: my publisher
Shain Jaffe—my agent at Great North Artists
Jerry Jordan—Jordan and Associates
Helen Kostick—my Mom, ongoing character and inspiration on *What's for Dinner?* She taught me everything about cooking.
Benny and Pearl—my adorable dogs, both of whom also make guest appearances on the show

"Keep on rattling those pots and pans!"

—CATH AND MICHAEL

COTE ST. LUC, QUEBEC

"Thank you for bringing some spice to our table."

—HILDI

BURNABY, BRITISH COLUMBIA

"You show us that anyone can prepare a delicious meal in half an hour, and it's not wieners and beans!"

—CORINA

WINNIPEG, MANITOBA

Introduction: The Very Best of Years

When people ask me to describe *What's for Dinner?* I invariably tag it as a television show that combines humour and food. But that's not the way it was meant to be! Initially, when the show was to air on the Life Network in 1994, it was touted as a "generic" daily cooking show; in this context, "generic" means a straightforward half hour of cooking presided over by an attractive female host and her irresistible male counterpart! Each episode's menu showcased dinner only. All dinners had to be cooked in 30 minutes or less, in real time—no prepping of food allowed; no done-to-perfection roast on the sidelines, awaiting its cue to magically appear. Another important aspect was that all the ingredients had to be readily available from the local grocer or supermarket. This was to be everyday cooking all dressed up. To round it out, *What's for Dinner?* would be spiced with healthy and low-fat tips, as well as nutritional tidbits about the ingredients featured in each recipe.

What happened? Unexpectedly, Life Network found themselves with the oddest couple in the kitchen perhaps since Felix and Oscar (naturally, Mary Jo was Oscar to my Felix). In very little time, the relationship Mary Jo and I established on camera was comic, playfully combative and often silly. Sometimes it was slapstick. By the third season, some would argue, it had crossed over to the "dark" side: no holds were barred! Dressing, cross-dressing, and rumours of cross-pollination—not!—increasingly made their way onto our unscripted set.

Elvis, bunnies, carrots and pilgrims: all were grist for our pepper mills. Dogs, mothers, sisters, brothers…they were roasted to perfection. It was bedlam and lambaste, all wrapped up in one neat package and skewered with a fork. Much to our surprise, the show was a breakaway success. Viewers responded enthusiastically as much to the quick-and-easy recipes as they did to the humour, which consisted of wisecracks, practical jokes and endless one-upmanship. In fact, the more we kibitzed, the higher our ratings soared. In no time, we were receiving 1,200 letters a week. Taking notice and taking aim, TV critics wrote a surfeit of articles, calling us a cult hit and a cross between Jerry Springer and Julia Child. Bullseye! And what fun it was. In the midst of all this attention, Mary Jo and I were nominated for a Gemini. Who'd have guessed?

Taping the show was strenuous. Every season, we shot 110 shows in six weeks, which translated into four or five shows a day! This no doubt explains why we often looked delirious (the later in the day the episode was filmed, the more delirious). As the show evolved, we introduced a live audience, celebrity guests, and—in season five—a cross-Canada tour. It was a blast! Accompanied by the entire cast and crew, we sometimes did our tapings and our shtick in front of audiences of 1,200 to 1,500. It was overwhelming, and gratifying.

Over the years, viewers have sent mail and e-mail consistently requesting recipes *and* commenting on the relationship between Mary Jo and me. They've been amused, entertained and often concerned about my well-being. Do I, for instance, get upset when Mary Jo mentions my toupée?! Okay, for the record, there is no toupée, wig or hair transplant: if you pull it, I will scream. The Big Girl's ongoing gag about my hair piece has gone too far—I still get letters from gentlemen across the country inquiring as to where I purchased my hair piece because, they write, it looks so real—she's pushing me over the edge!

I'm often asked, "What's it really like to work for Mary Jo?" If you must know, it's a treat. Her quick wit and unfailing ability to make me laugh means I looked forward to going to work every day that we taped *What's for Dinner?* I delighted in how far we pushed that envelope, although there were times even I was flabbergasted at what popped out on camera. (I've been known to face the camera and gasp, "I can't believe we just said that on national television!") It's that chutzpah, and of course the great food, that made the show so successful. Neither Mary Jo nor I were offended by the jokes and practical jokes we played on each other. Truth be told, we loved to shock each other, as well as our viewers.

Throughout this cookbook, some of those priceless moments (the practical jokes, the insults, the wackiness and the costume episodes) appear in snaps and anecdotes, as well as the best recipes culled from five seasons. Actually, all my recipes featured here have been updated—a little bit here, a little bit there. They reflect the great ideas all of us—including you, the viewers—have contributed. It's these variations on a theme that kept the show, and our dinners, current and delicious. *What's for Dinner?* you ask? Well, how about…

Appetizing Appetizers

From year 1, our first PR shot. (Always clowning around.)

Sliced Tomatoes and Fresh Basil with Mozzarella and Asiago Cheeses

SERVES 4 TO 6

Whenever I serve this, I picture myself dining outside a Tuscan villa overlooking a stunning panorama of mountains and orchards.

DRESSING

2 tbsp	olive oil
1 tbsp	wine vinegar
1	clove garlic, chopped

SALAD

2	large ripe tomatoes
6	large leaves fresh basil, chopped
½ cup	shredded mozzarella cheese
¼ cup	grated asiago cheese
½ tsp	black pepper

To make the dressing

Place the oil, vinegar and chopped garlic in a mixing bowl. Mix well.

To prepare the salad

Slice the tomatoes, not too thin, and place on a serving platter. Sprinkle with basil. Using a teaspoon, gently drizzle dressing over the tomato slices. Arrange mozzarella cheese on top of tomatoes and scatter the asiago cheese on top. Sprinkle with black pepper and serve.

Ya Gotta Love the Big Girl

During our slap-and-tickle cross-country tour, we sometimes got as many as 1,200 to 1,500 people showing up to watch a taping of *What's for Dinner?* on location. At a memorable taping in Montreal, I tripped and fell on-camera while tap dancing. Ignoring my mishap completely, Mary Jo continued talking to the camera, stepping right over me as she walked towards it. When I had finally picked myself up, dusted myself off, and stumbled towards Mary Jo, I said, "Thanks a lot for just stepping over me!" Her response was a mere, "You're lucky I didn't kick you as I went over." Mama Mia!

Chicken Bruschetta with Fresh Basil

SERVES 4 TO 6

Bruschetta is traditionally served "al pomodoro," which means with tomato, olive oil and garlic. This variation is an exceptional one.

Variation
Replace tomatoes with chopped zucchini.

1	stick French bread	1 tbsp	olive oil
1 cup	diced cooked chicken	1 tsp	lemon juice
4	small tomatoes, chopped	1 tsp	balsamic vinegar
2	cloves garlic, minced	1 tsp	black pepper
½ cup	chopped fresh parsley	½ cup	grated Cheddar cheese
½ cup	chopped fresh basil	¼ cup	grated Parmesan cheese
2 tbsp	Dijon mustard		

Slice the bread lengthwise and toast lightly in the oven. In a bowl, combine the chicken, tomatoes, garlic, parsley, basil, Dijon mustard, olive oil, lemon juice, balsamic vinegar and pepper. Spread tomato mixture over the toasted bread and sprinkle with Cheddar and Parmesan cheese. Broil for 2 to 3 minutes, until cheese has melted. Serve immediately.

Tip
You can use leftover chicken and day-old bread; it still tastes great.

Spicy Crabmeat Bruschetta with Red Wine

SERVES 4 TO 6

You could easily make this a Spicy Shrimp Bruschetta
by replacing the crab with 1/2 lb shrimp.

1	stick French bread	2 tbsp	Dijon mustard
3 tbsp	butter	2 tbsp	lemon juice
2	cloves garlic, minced	½ tsp	crushed red pepper flakes
½ cup	finely chopped celery	½ tsp	paprika
½	sweet red pepper, chopped	½ tsp	salt
½ lb	fresh crabmeat	½ tsp	black pepper
½ cup	chopped green onions	1	medium tomato, chopped
½ cup	chopped fresh parsley	1 tbsp	balsamic vinegar
¼ cup	red wine		

Slice the bread lengthwise and toast lightly in the oven. Remove bread from oven and cut each length into six pieces. Set aside. In a large sauté pan or skillet, melt the butter. Add garlic, then celery and sweet pepper, and sauté 2 minutes or until vegetables are tender. Stir in the crabmeat, green onions, parsley, red wine, Dijon mustard, lemon juice, red pepper flakes, paprika, salt and pepper. Simmer another 3 minutes. Add the tomato. Mix well and stir in the balsamic vinegar. Serve warm on the toasted French bread.

Calamari in Lemon Tomato Sauce

SERVES 4 TO 6

This was one of my Island specials, served on board
the Good Ship Lollipop.

Low-Fat Option
Sauté in 1/4 cup
vegetable stock
instead of oil.

Variation
Replace calamari with
jumbo shrimp or
scallops.

2 tbsp	olive oil	1/4 cup	chopped fresh coriander
2	cloves garlic, minced	1/4 cup	freshly squeezed lemon juice
1	large red onion, chopped		
3 cups	calamari rings	1 tbsp	lemon rind
4	medium tomatoes, chopped	1 tsp	brown sugar
1/2 cup	dry red wine	1/2 tsp	tomato paste
1/2 cup	orange juice		Lemon wedges for garnish
1/2 cup	water		

In a large sauté pan or skillet, heat the oil; sauté the garlic and onion for 2 to 3 minutes or until translucent. Add the calamari and sauté 3 to 4 minutes, until it turns white. Add the tomatoes, red wine, orange juice, water, coriander, lemon juice, lemon rind, brown sugar and tomato paste. Reduce heat to medium and simmer 8 to 10 minutes, until calamari is tender. Garnish with lemon wedges. Serve with French bread for dipping.

Sensational Salads of Every Sort

"Okay Mary Jo…keep smiling,
but get your hand outta there now!"

Watercress and Blue Cheese Salad

SERVES 4

During season three, Mary Jo and I, along with the crew of
What's for Dinner? *took a cruise to the Caribbean.*
This easy, simple watercress salad came out of that trip.

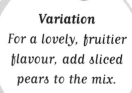

Variation
For a lovely, fruitier flavour, add sliced pears to the mix.

2	bunches watercress	1 tbsp	rice wine vinegar
3 tbsp	olive oil		Salt and pepper
1 tbsp	balsamic vinegar	½	cup crumbled blue cheese

Wash the watercress; blot dry with a paper towel and place in a salad bowl. Meanwhile, in a small mixing bowl, combine oil, balsamic vinegar, rice wine vinegar, salt and pepper; mix well. Pour over watercress and toss well. Add the blue cheese and serve immediately.

The Cruise

During our *What's for Dinner? on Location in the Caribbean* specials, I never let up playing practical jokes. I remember bribing the spa lady, who was to put a mud pack on Mary Jo, to do the deed and then leave her for more than the allotted 10 minutes. One hour and 15 minutes later, poor Mary Jo finally realized something was up, and left her cabin in peculiar make-up, looking for help. What patience!

Fennel and Goat Cheese Salad

SERVES 4

Goat cheese is the seventh wonder of the culinary world;
fennel the sixth.

DRESSING		SALAD	
1/4 cup	olive oil	1	medium fennel bulb, chopped
2 tbsp	lemon juice	1	medium cucumber, chopped
1 tsp	sugar	1	sweet red pepper, seeded and chopped
1 tsp	white wine vinegar	1/2 lb	mild goat cheese
1/2 tsp	black pepper	1/2 cup	freshly chopped parsley
		1/4 cup	freshly chopped mint

To make the dressing
In a medium salad bowl, combine the ingredients for the salad dressing: olive oil, lemon juice, sugar, vinegar and pepper. Mix well.

To prepare the salad
Place the chopped fennel, cucumber, red pepper, goat cheese, parsley and mint in a salad bowl. Pour dressing over salad; toss and serve.

Mixed Pepper and Avocado Salad

SERVES 4 TO 6

Colourful, crunchy strips of sweet bell pepper combine perfectly with wedges of smooth and creamy avocado for a wonderfully textured taste sensation.

DRESSING

2	cloves garlic, minced
1/4 cup	sour cream
2 tbsp	lemon juice
2 tbsp	olive oil
2 tbsp	balsamic vinegar
1 tbsp	Dijon mustard
1/2 tsp	cayenne
	Salt and pepper to taste

SALAD

2	tomatoes, cut into wedges
1	sweet red pepper, cut into strips
1	sweet yellow pepper, cut into strips
1	sweet green pepper, cut into strips
1	bunch asparagus, steamed and halved crosswise
1 cup	chopped fresh parsley
1/2 cup	chopped green onions
2	ripe avocados

To make the dressing

In a small mixing bowl, combine the garlic, sour cream, lemon juice, olive oil, balsamic vinegar, Dijon mustard, cayenne, salt and pepper. Whisk thoroughly until consistency is creamy.

To prepare the salad

In a salad bowl, combine the tomatoes, red pepper, yellow pepper, green pepper, asparagus, parsley and green onions. Just before serving, slice avocados, arrange atop salad and pour on dressing; toss well.

Sesame Grilled Vegetable Salad with Parmesan

SERVES 4 TO 6

*It was during my first season of **What's for Dinner?** that I
discovered the indoor grill: a fabulous invention. However,
it wasn't until my third season on the show that I discovered
this delicious salad—using my nifty indoor grill, of course.*

6	medium carrots, cut lengthwise and then crosswise into quarters	1	medium eggplant, sliced
		1	fennel bulb, sliced lengthwise
4	large portobello mushrooms, quartered	½ cup	sliced green onions
		¼ cup	sesame oil
4	ears of corn, halved crosswise	1	heart of romaine lettuce, chopped
2	medium zucchini, cut into strips	1 tbsp	sesame seeds
		2 tbsp	balsamic vinegar
2	sweet red peppers, chopped	½ cup	grated Parmesan cheese

Place carrots, mushrooms, corn, zucchini, peppers, eggplant, fennel and green
onions on paper towels; brush with sesame oil. On high heat, grill the vegetables
until tender but not overdone. Spread the romaine lettuce evenly on a large platter. Arrange the grilled vegetables on top. Sprinkle with sesame seeds. Drizzle with
balsamic vinegar and sprinkle with Parmesan. Serve immediately.

Low-Fat Coleslaw with Oranges and Almonds

SERVES 6 TO 8

A peppy variation on your favourite deli-style coleslaw.

DRESSING		SALAD	
¼ cup	orange juice, with pulp	4 cups	shredded cabbage
1 tbsp	light soy sauce	4	carrots, grated
1 tbsp	light mayonnaise	2	oranges, peeled, quartered and seeded
1 tbsp	balsamic vinegar	2	sweet red peppers, sliced thinly
1 tbsp	rice wine vinegar	1	medium red onion, sliced thinly
1 tbsp	lemon juice	½ cup	chopped fresh parsley
1 tbsp	orange rind	¼ cup	chopped fresh basil
¼ tsp	cayenne pepper	1 tbsp	orange rind
		2 tbsp	slivered almonds

To make the dressing

In a large jar, combine orange juice, soy sauce, mayonnaise, balsamic vinegar, rice wine vinegar, lemon juice, orange rind and cayenne pepper; shake until well mixed.

To prepare the salad

In a large mixing bowl, combine cabbage, carrots, oranges, red peppers, onion, parsley, basil and orange rind; toss well. Pour the dressing over the salad and toss again. Sprinkle with slivered almonds and serve.

My Favourite Fruit Salad

SERVES 4 TO 6

This season-three stand-out is not a dessert, although it tastes like one. Serve it with a grilled meat dish for your next backyard barbecue.

DRESSING

1 cup	yogurt
1/2 cup	sliced strawberries
1/2 cup	orange juice
1 tbsp	balsamic vinegar
2 tsp	honey
1 tsp	chopped fresh mint

SALAD

2	oranges, peeled and quartered
2	bananas, halved and sliced lengthwise
2	kiwifruit, peeled and sliced
2	pears, cored and sliced
1	grapefruit, peeled and cut into bite-size pieces
1	apple, sliced
1/2	honeydew melon, seeded and sliced
1 cup	halved strawberries
1 tsp	lemon juice
2 cups	watercress

To make the dressing

In a blender or food processor, purée the yogurt, strawberries, orange juice, balsamic vinegar, honey and mint until smooth.

To prepare the salad

In a large mixing bowl, combine the oranges, bananas, kiwifruit, pears, grapefruit, apple, melon and strawberries. Toss gently with lemon juice. Arrange the watercress on four salad plates. Starting from each plate's rim, arrange the fruit in a circular pattern, working toward the centre. Pour the dressing over the fruit, garnish each plate with mint leaves and serve.

Fusilli Salad with Combo Fruit and Vegetables

SERVES 4 TO 6

*A perfect dish for an **al fresco** lunch.*

SALAD		DRESSING	
4 cups	fusilli pasta	2	cloves garlic, minced
2 cups	chopped celery stalks	½ cup	orange juice
2	carrots, halved lengthwise and sliced	⅓ cup	olive oil
		¼ cup	chopped fresh basil
1	orange, peeled, seeded and quartered	2 tbsp	red wine vinegar
1	apple, chopped	1 tbsp	lemon juice
1	small red onion, chopped	1 tbsp	grated orange rind
1	sweet red pepper, chopped	½ tsp	salt
1	green pepper, chopped	½ tsp	pepper
½ cup	chopped fresh parsley		

To prepare the salad

In a large pot of boiling, slightly salted water, cook pasta for about 12 minutes or until tender but firm (al dente). Drain and return to pot. Add celery, carrots, orange, apple, onion, red pepper, green pepper and parsley; toss well.

To make the dressing

In a food processor, blend the garlic, orange juice, olive oil, basil, vinegar, lemon juice, orange rind, salt and pepper; purée until smooth. Pour dressing over salad and toss well. Chill 20 minutes before serving.

Penne Salad with Feta

SERVES 6

You can't go wrong with the Greek-inspired pasta salad.

4 cups	penne pasta, cooked	1 tsp	dried oregano
2	medium tomatoes, chopped	½ tsp	dried rosemary
1	small cucumber, diced	½ tsp	dried basil
1	sweet red pepper, diced	½ tsp	black pepper
1	green pepper, diced	2 tbsp	wine vinegar
1 cup	cooked, chopped green beans	2 tbsp	olive oil
1 cup	crumbled feta cheese	2 tbsp	Dijon mustard
		1 tsp	balsamic vinegar

In a large mixing bowl, combine the cooked penne, tomatoes, cucumber, red pepper, green pepper, green beans and feta. Sprinkle the oregano, rosemary and basil on top, and mix well. In a small mixing bowl, combine the black pepper, vinegar, oil, Dijon mustard and balsamic vinegar. Drizzle over the salad and serve.

Variation
Replace feta with a light goat cheese.

The Best Bean Salad

SERVES 6

*This is a fabulous salad, especially after it's spent
a night in the fridge.*

Variation
*Substitute 1/2 cup
chopped fresh coriander
for the parsley, and
replace the Dijon
mustard with a mild
curry paste.*

Variation
*Add medium cooked
shrimps to the
vegetables.*

½ cup	olive oil		1 cup	chick-peas
3 tbsp	lemon juice		1 cup	black beans
1 tsp	white wine vinegar		1 cup	white lima beans
1 tbsp	Dijon mustard		1	red pepper, chopped
½ tsp	dried basil		1	yellow pepper, chopped
½ tsp	dried thyme		1 cup	chopped fresh parsley
½ tsp	dried oregano		½ cup	chopped green onions
½ tsp	black pepper		1 tsp	lemon rind

In a medium mixing bowl, combine the oil, lemon juice, vinegar, Dijon mustard, basil, thyme, oregano and pepper; mix well. Add the chick-peas, black beans, lima beans, red pepper, yellow pepper, parsley and green onions. Mix well and refrigerate 30 minutes. Just before serving, sprinkle with lemon rind; mix and serve.

Seafood Salad with Lemon Vinaigrette

SERVES 6

*It's the uncomplicated, fresh flavours of the seafood
combined with citrus that make it so yummy.*

Variation
*Substitute swordfish
cut into 1-inch cubes
for the scallops.*

SEAFOOD		DRESSING	
2 cups	dry white wine	½ cup	olive oil
	Juice of 1 lemon		Juice of 2 lemons
2 tbsp	chopped fresh dill	2 tbsp	white wine vinegar
2	cloves garlic, chopped	1	clove garlic, chopped
16	medium scallops	1 tsp	chopped fresh dill
12	medium shrimp, cleaned	1 tsp	black pepper
	and deveined	1 tsp	dried basil
1 can	(10 oz) clams, drained		
1 can	(6 oz) crabmeat, drained		

To prepare the seafood
In a large frying pan or sauté pan, combine the wine, lemon juice, dill and garlic.
Bring the liquid to a boil and reduce to a simmer. Add the scallops, shrimp and
clams. Simmer about 4 minutes, or until the scallops turn white and the shrimp
turns pink. Remove the seafood. Place in a large salad bowl and add the crabmeat.
Allow the seafood to chill at least 1 hour in the refrigerator.

To prepare the dressing
In a small mixing bowl, combine the oil, lemon juice, vinegar, garlic, dill, black
pepper and basil. Mix the dressing well.

To put together the salad
Once the seafood has cooled, combine with dressing and serve. The salad should
be served chilled but not too cold.

Scallop, Fennel and Mint Salad

SERVES 4

*Ah, fennel...this refreshing salad appeared in season four—
my scandalous "preference" for fennel was, by then,
a source of some gossip!*

Variation
*Replace the scallop
with 24 medium
cooked shrimp.*

3 cups	cooked medium scallops	2	heads of Boston lettuce
1	small fennel bulb, sliced thinly	3 tbsp	white wine vinegar
1	medium red onion, sliced thinly	2 tbsp	olive oil
½ cup	chopped fresh parsley	½ tsp	dried basil
¼ cup	fresh mint leaves	½ tsp	dried thyme
		½ tsp	black pepper

In a medium mixing bowl, combine the scallops, fennel, onion, parsley and mint. Mix well. Line the inside of a salad bowl with the Boston lettuce. Place scallop mixture inside. In a small mixing bowl, combine the vinegar, oil, basil, thyme and black pepper. Mix well, drizzle over the salad and serve.

Grilled Sesame Steak and Two-Bean Salad

SERVES 6

*This meal can be vegetarian: just replace the steak with
large grilled portobello mushrooms.*

3 tbsp	sesame oil	½ lb	fresh green beans, cut
2 tbsp	olive oil	½ lb	fresh yellow beans, cut
1 tbsp	balsamic vinegar	2	romaine lettuces,
2 tsp	rice wine vinegar		hearts only
1 tsp	lemon juice	1 cup	halved cherry tomatoes
1 tsp	black pepper	1 tsp	sesame seeds
½ tsp	chili powder		
1 lb	round steak, 1 inch thick, fat trimmed		

Variation
*Replace the steak
with grilled chicken.*

In a small mixing bowl, combine 2 tbsp of the sesame oil, olive oil, balsamic vinegar, rice wine vinegar, lemon juice, 1/2 tsp of the pepper and chili powder. Mix well and set aside. Using the remaining 1 tbsp sesame oil, gently brush the steak and sprinkle the remaining 1/2 tsp pepper on both sides. Grill on high heat until grill marks appear, about 3 minutes each side for medium, longer for well-done. Remove and allow to cool. In a sauté pan, blanch the green and yellow beans for about 4 minutes, then rinse with cold water and drain. Cut the steak into thin strips. On a large serving platter, arrange the lettuce and then place the steak and beans on top; surround by the cherry tomatoes. Drizzle dressing over salad and sprinkle with sesame seeds.

Grilled New York Steak Salad with Garlic Mustard Sauce

SERVES 4

This delicious, hearty meal-in-a-salad was a fifth-season favourite. Enjoy.

Variation
Substitute chicken breasts for the steaks.

STEAKS
1 tbsp	black pepper
1 tsp	onion powder
1 tsp	chili powder
½ tsp	dried basil
2	6-oz New York steaks

DRESSING
½	cup yogurt
3 tbsp	Dijon mustard
4	cloves garlic, minced
1 tbsp	balsamic vinegar
1 tbsp	lemon juice
1 tsp	Worcestershire sauce
½ tsp	dried oregano

SALAD
2	romaine lettuce hearts, torn into pieces
1	small red onion, thinly sliced
8	cherry tomatoes

To prepare steaks
Combine 1/2 tbsp of the pepper, onion powder, chili powder and basil. Mix well and sprinkle evenly on the steaks. Using an indoor or outdoor grill, place the steaks over high heat and sear both sides. Grill as desired. Remove and slice thinly.

To make the dressing
Combine the yogurt, Dijon mustard, garlic, balsamic vinegar, lemon juice, Worcestershire sauce, oregano and the remaining 1/2 tbsp black pepper in a blender; blend until smooth.

To put together the salad
Place the romaine lettuce, onion and cherry tomatoes on a deep serving platter, place the steak on the salad and top with dressing.

Steak, Asparagus and Avocado Salad

SERVES 4 TO 6

Serve this salad, instead of vegetables, as a side dish.

DRESSING		SALAD	
1	ripened avocado	3	tomatoes, cut into wedges
4	cloves garlic, minced	1	sweet red pepper, cut in strips
2	tbsp sour cream	1	sweet yellow pepper, cut in strips
2	tbsp lemon juice	1	bunch asparagus, steamed and halved, crosswise
2	tbsp olive oil		
1	tbsp Dijon mustard		
½ tsp	cayenne pepper	½ cup	chopped green onions
	Salt and pepper to taste	½ cup	canned red beans
		½ cup	chopped fresh parsley
		2	ripened avocados
		2 cups	sliced grilled beef

Variation
Replace the beef with 2 cups sliced grilled chicken or turkey breasts.

Low-Fat Option
Replace the sour cream with yogurt.

To prepare dressing

Peel, pit and mash avocado. In a small mixing bowl, combine avocado, garlic, sour cream, lemon juice, olive oil, Dijon mustard, cayenne pepper, salt and pepper. Whisk until smooth. Set aside.

To prepare salad

In a salad bowl, combine the tomatoes, red pepper, yellow pepper, asparagus, green onions, beans and parsley. Just before serving, peel, pit and slice the 2 avocados. Place the avocados and sliced beef on the salad. Pour on the dressing and toss well. Serve immediately.

Grilled Steak and Grapefruit Watercress Salad

SERVES 2

This is a delicious, tangy salad that, if served to two, is truly a meal in itself.

MARINADE
½ cup	grapefruit juice, with pulp
½ cup	soy sauce
2	cloves garlic, minced
2 tbsp	orange rind
1 tsp	hot horseradish
½ tsp	dried thyme
½ tsp	dried basil
½ tsp	black pepper
1	10-oz sirloin steak, fat trimmed
1	large grapefruit, thickly sliced crosswise

DRESSING
¼ cup	grapefruit juice
2 tbsp	olive oil
1 tbsp	finely chopped grapefruit rind
1 tsp	balsamic vinegar
1 tsp	Worcestershire sauce
1 tsp	Dijon mustard
½ tsp	black pepper
2	cloves garlic, minced

SALAD
4 cups	watercress
8	cherry tomatoes

To prepare steak and grapefruit

In a bowl, whisk together the grapefruit juice, soy sauce, garlic, orange rind, horseradish, thyme, basil and pepper. Set aside 3 tbsp of the marinade. Marinate steak, covered and refrigerated, for at least 2 hours. When ready, grill or broil the steak 8 minutes for rare and 15 minutes for well-done, occasionally basting with the reserved marinade. Slice and set aside. Meanwhile, grill or broil the grapefruit slices until browned. Remove and let cool.

To make the dressing

In a small mixing bowl, combine the grapefruit juice, oil, rind, vinegar, Worcestershire sauce, Dijon mustard, black pepper and garlic; mix well.

To put together the salad

On a platter, arrange watercress, grapefruit slices and tomatoes. Top with beef slices; drizzle with dressing. Serve immediately.

Year 2: The Wrap Party. They called me "L'il Elvis."

Saucy Sauces, Divine Vinaigrettes and One Ravishing Relish

Cast Photo #1: All ready now.

Apple and Cinnamon Sauce

MAKES 1 CUP

This tasty sauce is great with pork, beef, chicken or fish.

2	apples, peeled, cored and chopped	½ cup	sour cream
½ cup	apple juice	1 tsp	soy sauce
½ cup	yogurt	1 tsp	balsamic vinegar
½ tsp	cinnamon	½ tsp	dried basil
		½ tsp	black pepper

In a saucepan, combine the apples and apple juice and cook for 10 minutes or until the chopped apple has softened. Using a hand mixer, purée until smooth. Add the yogurt and cinnamon. Mix until smooth, about 2 minutes. Add the sour cream and continue to mix another 2 minutes. Add soy sauce, vinegar, basil and black pepper. Mix over low heat about 4 minutes or until smooth. Serve warm.

Lemon Parsley Vinaigrette

MAKES 1 CUP

This delicious, easy vinaigrette—which made its first appearance sometime during our fourth-season shenanigans—is terrific on any green salad.

1/4 cup	olive oil		1/2 tsp	black pepper
1/4 cup	chopped fresh parsley		1/2 tsp	dried thyme
4 tbsp	lemon juice		1 tsp	balsamic vinegar
2	cloves garlic, minced		1 tsp	wine vinegar
2	tbsp grated lemon rind		1/4 tsp	sea salt

In a blender or using a hand mixer, combine the olive oil, parsley, lemon juice, garlic, lemon rind, black pepper, thyme, balsamic vinegar, wine vinegar and sea salt; purée for 2 minutes or until smooth. Keep refrigerated and shake prior to using.

Cast Photo #2: Not ready.

Strawberry and Mint Salad Dressing

MAKES 1 CUP

As well as on salads, use this dressing to baste fish, meat,
poultry or vegetables when grilling or roasting.

Variation
Replace the strawberries
with peeled, cored and
chopped ripe pear; if you
do, replace the apple juice
with grape or
pear juice.

¾ cup	sliced fresh strawberries	2 tbsp	lemon juice
½ cup	yogurt	2 tbsp	grated lemon rind
½ cup	chopped fresh parsley	2 tbsp	olive oil
½ cup	apple juice	2 tbsp	white wine vinegar
¼ cup	chopped fresh mint	2 tbsp	liquid honey

In a blender or with a hand blender, purée the strawberries, yogurt, parsley, apple juice, mint, lemon juice, lemon rind, olive oil, vinegar and honey.

The Most Excellent Strawberry Dressing

MAKES 1 1/2 CUPS

*The title doesn't lie: this is truly a stand-out that should be
tried at least once. What you serve it with is up to you,
but try it with romaine lettuce. Good eating!*

¾ cup	fresh strawberries		1 tsp	liquid honey
½ cup	yogurt		1 tsp	dried tarragon
¼ cup	olive oil		¼ cup	sliced strawberries
2 tbsp	vinegar			for garnish
1 tbsp	lemon juice			Ground black pepper
1	clove garlic, minced			to taste

Rinse strawberries in a colander. In a blender, or using a hand-held mixer, purée
strawberries, yogurt, oil, vinegar, lemon juice, garlic, honey and tarragon until
thick but not liquid. Drizzle dressing over a bed of lettuce and toss. Garnish with
sliced strawberries and ground pepper.

Tip
*When serving on
romaine lettuce, toss
1/2 cup croutons
with the salad after
the dressing is
added.*

Red Pepper, Honey and Mint Relish

MAKES 1 CUP

I use sweet red peppers, not the hot ones, for this relish, which is a great accompaniment for fish, pasta or just about anything. To serve hot, place it in a sauce pan and allow to simmer 10 minutes. If liquid reduces too much, add more stock or—for a sweeter taste—more apple juice.

4	medium red peppers, chopped	½ cup	apple juice
1	medium red onion, chopped	¼ cup	chopped fresh mint
1	cup vegetable stock	¼ cup	liquid honey
		½ tsp	black pepper

Combine the red peppers, onion, stock, juice, mint, honey and pepper in a food processor; purée until smooth. Serve cold over fish, meat or poultry.

Does Jiminy Cricket come to mind?

Kenny's Low-Fat Tomato Sauce

MAKES 4 CUPS

*Whether you say t-"oh"-mato or t-"ah"-mato, this sauce
is easy and healthy—what could be better?!*

1	can (28 oz) stewed tomatoes		½ cup	chopped fresh parsley
1 cup	tomato juice		¼ cup	chopped fresh oregano or ½ tsp dried
1 cup	apple juice		2	cloves garlic, chopped
1	medium onion, chopped		2 tbsp	tomato paste
½ cup	chopped mushrooms		1 tsp	salt
½ cup	diced carrots		1 tsp	black pepper
½ cup	diced red pepper		½ tsp	hot sauce
½ cup	diced green or yellow pepper		1	bay leaf

In a large saucepan, combine the stewed tomatoes, tomato juice, apple juice, onion, mushrooms, carrots, red pepper, green or yellow pepper, parsley, oregano, garlic, tomato paste, salt, pepper, hot sauce and bay leaf. Bring to a boil; reduce to low heat and simmer 15 to 20 minutes or until the liquid is reduced by half. If it reduces too much, add more tomato juice. Remove and discard the bay leaf. Serve with cooked pasta.

Pesto Sauce

MAKES 1 CUP

Pesto is traditionally used with pasta, but try this low-fat version to dress a salad.

Tip
To use as a pasta sauce, add cooked pasta to hot pesto and cook another minute. Serve immediately.

2 cups	fresh basil	2 tbsp	pine nuts
4	cloves garlic	2 tbsp	Dijon mustard
1 cup	vegetable stock	½ tsp	sea salt
1 cup	chopped mushrooms	½ tsp	black pepper
¼ cup	grated Parmesan cheese		

In a blender or food processor combine the basil, garlic, stock, mushrooms, Parmesan cheese, pine nuts, Dijon mustard, salt and pepper. Blend until smooth. Transfer to a large sauté pan and simmer until reduced by half, about 5 minutes.

On-Camera Hi-Jinks

The great thing about working on *What's for Dinner?* was that we would never know what either of us would do on camera. Mary Jo certainly never knew when I might

- step on her foot behind the counter
- steal her utensils
- hide her cookbook
- have sauce on my hands and smear her with it
- trip her (before she'd trip me!)

Low-Fat Honey Mustard Sauce

MAKES 1 CUP

*This wonderful sauce contains approximately 22 calories
per tablespoon.*

1/4 cup	vegetable stock		1/4 cup	Dijon mustard
2	cloves garlic, finely chopped		1 tbsp	balsamic vinegar
			1/2 tsp	dried thyme
1/4 cup	non-fat sour cream		1/2 tsp	ground black pepper
1/4 cup	non-fat yogurt		2 tbsp	liquid honey

Using a saucepan, heat the stock and sauté the garlic in it about 2 minutes. Add the sour cream and mix well over heat, about 2 minutes. Add the yogurt, Dijon mustard, balsamic vinegar, thyme and black pepper. Continue to stir over heat about 5 minutes, allowing the sauce to reduce by about one-third. Add the honey and mix. Serve warm over beef, chicken or pork.

Dill and Parsley Dressing

MAKES 1 CUP

*This herbal dressing was first tested during the fourth season of **What's for Dinner?**: it got the thumbs-up from the cast, the crew, the audience—and Pearl.*

Variation
If you want to use this as a marinade, add an extra 1 cup of vegetable stock.

½ cup	vegetable stock		2 tbsp	lemon juice
½ cup	yogurt		2 tbsp	balsamic vinegar
½ cup	chopped fresh dill		½ tsp	black pepper
¼ cup	chopped fresh parsley		½ tsp	sea salt
2	cloves garlic			

Using a hand blender or blender, combine the stock, yogurt, dill, parsley, garlic, lemon juice, balsamic vinegar, pepper and salt; purée until smooth. Serve over romaine lettuce.

Balsamic Vinaigrette with Goat Cheese

MAKES 1/2 CUP

*Serve this delicious vinaigrette on a salad of arugula,
radicchio, endive, or whichever greens you prefer.*

1/4 cup	olive oil (preferably extra virgin)
1/4 cup	chopped onion
1	clove garlic, finely chopped
1/4 cup	balsamic vinegar
2 tbsp	Dijon Mustard
1/4 cup	crumbled goat cheese
1 tsp	salt

In a skillet, heat oil. Toss in the onion and sauté for 4 to 5 minutes, or until lightly browned. Stir in the garlic and sauté for another 2 to 3 minutes. Add the balsamic vinegar and Dijon mustard and simmer, allowing to reduce by half. Add the goat cheese and salt. Remove from heat and serve over greens.

Probably a joke not suitable for national TV...like that matters!

Kenny's Low-Fat Caesar Salad Dressing with Fresh Basil

MAKES 1 CUP

One of my most popular recipes is a No-Mayo,
No-Oil Caesar dressing, which appeared on the first season
*of **What's for Dinner?** This "variation on a variation" is even*
tastier. Enjoy it with romaine lettuce and croutons,
and without loads of fat or calories: there are only 29 calories
and .7 grams of fat per tablespoon.

Variation
Replace the non-fat sour cream with non-fat yogurt.

¾ cup	non-fat sour cream		1 tbsp	lemon juice
¼ cup	chopped fresh basil		1 tbsp	balsamic vinegar
¼ cup	grated Parmesan cheese		1 tsp	anchovy paste or
4	cloves garlic, minced			1 anchovy, mashed
2 tbsp	Worcestershire sauce		½ tsp	black pepper
1 tbsp	low-sodium soy sauce		½ tsp	chili powder

In a blender or using a hand blender, puree the sour cream, basil, Parmesan cheese, garlic, Worcestershire sauce, soy sauce, lemon juice, balsamic vinegar, anchovy, pepper and chili powder until smooth. Serve over romaine lettuce torn apart: 2 heads if using only the heart sections, or 1 head if using all of it.

Caesar Salad Dressing Number "9"

MAKES 1 CUP

Okay, this isn't really my 9th Caesar dressing, but it could be—
I'm always experimenting. This one happens to be truer
to the original.

¼ cup	sour cream	2 tbsp	lemon juice
¼ cup	grated Parmesan cheese	2 tbsp	white wine vinegar
3 tbsp	olive oil	1 tsp	Worcestershire sauce
4	cloves garlic, minced	½ tsp	anchovy paste
1	shallot, minced	½ tsp	black pepper

In a food processor, combine the sour cream, Parmesan cheese, olive oil, garlic, shallot, lemon juice, wine vinegar, Worcestershire sauce, anchovy paste and black pepper; purée until smooth.

Tip
This dressing will keep covered in the refrigerator for about a week.

Hot and Steamy
Soups Galore

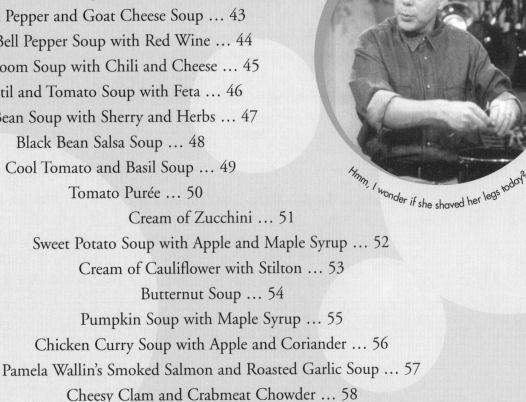

Hmm, I wonder if she shaved her legs today?

Low-Fat Option
Use low-fat or non-fat yogurt and light coconut milk.

Chilled Pineapple Soup with Coconut

SERVES 4 TO 6

This sweet soup is inspired by the islands of the Caribbean, many of which Mary Jo and I visited for our one-hour TV specials.

4 cups	chopped pineapple	½ cup	unsweetened coconut flakes
4 cups	pineapple juice		
1 cup	yogurt	½ cup	chopped fresh parsley
1 cup	orange juice	½ tsp	ground cinnamon
1 cup	coconut milk	½ tsp	black pepper

Using a blender or food processor, combine the pineapple, pineapple juice, yogurt, orange juice, coconut milk, coconut flakes, parsley, cinnamon and black pepper; purée until smooth. Allow to chill in the refrigerator at least an hour prior to serving. Sprinkle on a little cinnamon as garnish.

The Cruise II

I have so many fond memories of our Caribbean cruise. One thing I enjoyed was spiking poor unsuspecting Mary Jo's piña coladas—until I realized that she was enjoying herself far too much. After that, I paid the bartenders to serve her virgin piña coladas only. I'm such a killjoy. Tee hee!

Garlic Soup with Coriander and Parmesan

SERVES 6 TO 8

*This soup—which calls for 24 garlic cloves!—is as healthy
as it is delicious.*

7 cups	vegetable stock	1 tbsp	Dijon mustard
24	garlic cloves, chopped	½ tsp	dried basil
2	potatoes, peeled and cubed	½ tsp	salt
1	medium onion, chopped	½ tsp	white pepper
1 cup	white wine	¼ cup	grated Parmesan cheese
½ cup	finely chopped fresh coriander		

In a large soup pot, bring the stock to a boil. Reduce to a simmer. Add the garlic, potatoes, onion, wine, 1/4 cup of the coriander, Dijon mustard, basil, salt and pepper. Simmer, covered, about 15 minutes or until potatoes are cooked. Using a hand blender, blend the soup until smooth. Add the remaining 1/4 cup coriander and Parmesan cheese and serve.

French Onion Soup with White Wine

SERVES 4 TO 6

*This recipe calls for slices of French bread, toasted darkly,
but don't despair if it isn't available. You can use other
types of bread; just use a cookie cutter to cut it into
a smaller, round slice.*

4 tbsp	olive oil	½ tsp	dried rosemary
2	red onions, sliced	½ tsp	dried oregano
2	onions, sliced	½ tsp	salt
8 cups	beef stock or vegetable stock	½ tsp	black pepper
½ cup	white wine	6	thick slices French bread, toasted
2 tbsp	Dijon mustard	1 cup	mozzarella cheese, shredded
1 tbsp	balsamic vinegar	½ cup	chopped fresh parsley
½ tsp	dried sweet basil		

In a large soup pot, heat oil. Add onions and sauté in bunches until brown, about
15 minutes. Add the stock, wine, Dijon mustard, balsamic vinegar, basil, rosemary,
oregano, salt and pepper. Bring to a boil and reduce to a simmer for about 10 minutes. Ladle into 4 to 6 oven-proof soup bowls. Place a slice of toasted French bread
on top of each bowl. Sprinkle each toast with cheese and place bowls in the oven,
on the grill, for 3 to 4 minutes, or until the cheese melts and starts to turn brown.
Serve immediately with fresh parley on top.

Red Pepper and Goat Cheese Soup

SERVES 4 TO 6

The goat cheese, which is added last to this pepper pot soup,
adds a lovely, creamy texture.

2 tbsp	olive oil	½ tsp	cayenne
1	large onion, chopped	½ tsp	salt
3	red peppers, chopped	½ tsp	black pepper
5 cups	vegetable stock	½ cup	goat cheese
1 tbsp	lemon juice	2 tsp	chopped fresh coriander

In a large pot, heat oil. Add onion and sauté for 2 to 3 minutes or until translucent. Add peppers and sauté another 2 minutes. Pour in stock and bring to a boil. Reduce heat to simmer and stir in lemon juice, cayenne, salt and pepper. Continue simmering for 10 minutes. Using a hand blender, purée soup until smooth. Stir in goat cheese and coriander and serve.

Variation
If you don't have coriander, feel free to use chopped fresh parsley.

Oh no! The burner's not on...I'll just keep smiling

Red Bell Pepper Soup with Red Wine

SERVES 4 TO 6

*No doubt about it: this soup is red hot! And Brian Orser,
the guest on **What's for Dinner?** that day, agreed!*

Low-Fat Option
*Leave out the table cream
and add 1 extra cup of
vegetable stock. For a
creamier texture, add 2
cooked potatoes to the
vegetable stock.*

2 tbsp	olive oil		2 tbsp	chopped fresh basil
1	medium onion, chopped		1 tbsp	chopped fresh thyme
4	sweet red peppers, chopped		1 tsp	brown sugar
6 cups	vegetable stock		½ tsp	paprika
½ cup	red wine		½ tsp	chili powder
2	plum tomatoes, chopped		½ tsp	salt
1	bay leaf		½ tsp	black pepper
			1 cup	table cream

In a large soup pot, heat the oil. Add the onion and sauté for 2 to 3 minutes or until translucent. Add the red peppers and sauté another 2 to 3 minutes or until tender. Add the vegetable stock, red wine, tomatoes, bay leaf, basil, thyme, brown sugar, paprika, chili powder, salt and pepper. Bring to a boil; reduce heat and simmer 20 minutes, stirring occasionally. Discard bay leaf. Using a hand blender, or in a food processor, blend the soup until it has a creamy consistency. If using a food processor, return blended soup to the pot. Slowly fold in cream. Heat through and serve immediately.

Mushroom Soup with Chili and Cheese

SERVES 4 TO 6

*This hearty soup is a meal within a meal: serve it
with bread and hops (beer)!*

3 tbsp	olive oil	½ tsp	dried thyme
1	medium onion, chopped	½ tsp	paprika
1	cloves garlic, finely chopped	½ tsp	salt
		½ tsp	black pepper
5 cups	chopped button mushrooms	¼ tsp	cayenne pepper
7 cups	vegetable stock	1 cup	mashed potatoes
1 tsp	chili powder	2	tomatoes, diced
½ tsp	dried oregano	1 cup	cream
		½ cup	shredded Cheddar cheese

In a large soup pot, heat the oil. Add the onion and garlic and sauté for 2 to 3 minutes or until onion is translucent. Add the mushrooms and sauté for another 8 to 10 minutes. Pour in the vegetable stock and bring to a boil. Reduce heat to simmer and add the chili powder, oregano, thyme, paprika, salt, pepper and cayenne. Cook for about 5 minutes and then add the potato and tomatoes. Simmer for 20 minutes on low. Using a hand mixer, purée the soup to a nice creamy texture. Add the cream and cheese and mix well on the stove another 5 minutes.

Variation
*Replace button
mushrooms with different
types like oyster and
portobello—this adds
a richer flavour.*

Low-Fat Option
*Replace the cream
with skim milk and
the cheese with a
low-fat version.*

Tip
*If liquid reduces too
much, add more
vegetable stock.*

Lentil and Tomato Soup with Feta

SERVES 4 TO 6

This fifth-season wonder got raves from viewers.

Variation
Replace the fresh tomatoes with 4 medium potatoes, boiled or mashed.

Tip
If using the dried lentils, soak them overnight or for several hours covered with water in a bowl.

6 cups	vegetable stock		2	cloves garlic, finely chopped
2 cups	cooked lentils		½ tsp	dried rosemary
1 can	(28 oz) crushed tomatoes		½ tsp	dried oregano
1	large plum tomato, chopped		½ tsp	black pepper
1	small cooking onion, chopped		1	bay leaf
½ cup	chopped fresh parsley		½ cup	crumbled feta cheese

In a large soup pot, combine the stock, lentils, tomatoes, onion, 1/4 cup of the parsley, garlic, rosemary, oregano, black pepper and the bay leaf. Bring to a boil and reduce to a simmer. Simmer about 25 minutes. Remove the bay leaf. With a hand mixer, purée the ingredients until the soup has a creamy texture. Serve immediately and garnish with feta cheese and the remaining 1/4 cup parsley.

Black Bean Soup with Sherry and Herbs

SERVES 4 TO 6

*This is delicious as a soup but, if you want a
real Southwestern-style gumbo, add 1 cup sliced and
blanched okra and serve it over rice.*

2 tbsp	olive oil	1	bay leaf
2	cloves garlic, finely chopped	6 cups	vegetable stock
1	medium white onion, finely chopped	4 cups	cooked black beans
		2 tbsp	balsamic vinegar
2 tbsp	chopped fresh thyme	2 tbsp	dry sherry
2 tbsp	chopped fresh rosemary	½ tsp	black pepper
1 tsp	jalapeño pepper, seeded and finely chopped	½ tsp	salt
		¼ cup	chopped fresh parsley

In a large soup pot, heat the oil over medium heat. Add the garlic, onion, thyme, rosemary, jalapeño pepper and bay leaf. Sauté for 3 to 4 minutes or until onion is golden. Stir in the stock, black beans and balsamic vinegar. Increase heat to medium-high and bring soup to a boil, stirring frequently to prevent the beans from sticking to the bottom of the pot. As the soup begins to boil, slowly stir in the sherry. Add salt and pepper. Stir well and remove from heat. Sprinkle with parsley; stir well, and serve.

Variation
*If sherry is not
available, any red or
white wine will do.*

Low-Fat Option
*Replace the olive oil
with a vegetable oil.*

Tip
*If you are using
dried black beans, soak
in water overnight (allow
3 cups of water for every
cup of beans); in the morning, drain, rinse
and begin the
recipe.*

Black Bean Salsa Soup

SERVES 4 TO 6

Ahhhh! The salsa-samba variation of my bean soup...
I love the zip of hot salsa in all my soups.
Serve this with nachos.

Low-Fat Option
Use 2 tbsp of vegetable stock instead of olive oil when sautéing.

2 tbsp	olive oil		2 tbsp	chopped fresh basil
1	medium white onion, finely chopped		1 tbsp	chili powder
			½ tsp	salt
2	celery stalks, chopped		½ tsp	black pepper
2	cloves garlic, finely chopped		1	bay leaf
			4 cups	cooked black beans
6 cups	vegetable stock		½ cup	cooked corn
1 cup	mild or hot salsa		¼ cup	chopped fresh parsley
1 cup	tomato juice		2 tbsp	sour cream
¼ cup	chopped fresh dill		½ cup	chopped fresh chives
¼ cup	chopped fresh coriander			

In a large soup pot, heat the oil over medium heat. Sauté onion and celery in hot oil for 1 minute. Add the garlic and sauté for another 2 minutes or until onion is translucent. Stir in the stock, salsa, tomato juice, dill, coriander, basil, chili powder, salt, pepper and bay leaf. Bring to a boil; reduce heat and simmer uncovered, stirring occasionally, for 20 minutes. Stir in black beans and corn; cook another 2 minutes. Add the parsley and mix well. Discard the bay leaf. Serve in bowls, garnished with a dollop of sour cream and chives.

Cool Tomato and Basil Soup

SERVES 4 TO 6

*This is great on a hot summer's day. Serve cold as a starter
with something grilled, or as a whole meal with a salad.*

4 cups	vegetable stock	1/4 cup	chopped fresh dill
1 can	(28 oz) chopped stewed tomatoes	1	medium onion, chopped
4	ripe tomatoes, chopped	2	cloves garlic, chopped
1 cup	table cream	2	celery stalks, chopped
3/4 cup	chopped fresh basil	1 tsp	dried basil
1/2 cup	tomato juice	1/2 tsp	salt
		1/2 tsp	black pepper

In a large bowl combine the stock, tomatoes, cream, basil, tomato juice, dill,
onion, garlic, celery, basil, salt and pepper. Using a hand blender, or in a food
processor, purée until smooth. If using a food processor, return the soup to the
bowl. Refrigerate, covered, for at least 1 hour prior
to serving. Serve cold in soup bowls.

Variation
*Substitute fresh
coriander for the dill.*

I'm sorry, but you really can't look at these right now.

Tomato Purée

This is a wonderful, light, low-fat tomato soup;
serve with a green salad and Italian herbed bread.

2 tbsp	canola oil		1	bay leaf
1	large onion, chopped		1/2 tsp	dried basil
1	clove garlic, minced		1/2 tsp	dried oregano
5 cups	vegetable stock		1/2 tsp	salt
1 can	(28 oz) stewed tomatoes		1/2 tsp	black pepper
4	tomatoes, chopped		1/4 tsp	chili powder
1 cup	tomato juice		1 cup	mashed potatoes
1/4 cup	chopped fresh parsley		1/2 cup	chopped watercress
1 tbsp	tomato paste			

In a large, heavy saucepan, heat oil. Sauté onion and garlic in oil for 2 to 3 minutes, or until onion is translucent. Add stock, tomatoes, tomato juice, parsley, tomato paste, bay leaf, basil, oregano, salt, pepper and chili powder. Bring to a boil. Reduce heat and simmer uncovered, stirring occasionally, about 20 minutes. Discard bay leaf. Add the mashed potatoes and mix gently. Purée the mixture to a creamy texture. Garnish with watercress and serve.

Cream of Zucchini

SERVES 6 TO 8

*Here's a way to turn a garden-variety squash
into something quite sophisticated.*

2 tbsp	olive oil		½ cup	red wine
1	medium cooking onion, chopped		1	small potato, cubed
1	clove garlic, chopped		1	red pepper, chopped
6 cups	vegetable stock		1 tbsp	dried parsley
4	medium zucchini, cubed small		½ tsp	dried basil
			½ tsp	dried rosemary
1 cup	table cream		½ tsp	dried thyme
1 cup	milk		½ tsp	black pepper
			1	bay leaf

In a large non-stick soup pot, heat oil. Sauté onion and garlic in oil for 2 to 3 minutes or until translucent. Add the stock, zucchini, cream, milk, wine, potato, red pepper, parsley, basil, rosemary, thyme, black pepper and bay leaf. Bring to a boil and reduce to simmer. Simmer about 20 minutes or until zucchini and potatoes are cooked. Remove bay leaf; with hand mixer purée the soup and serve immediately. If the soup is too thick, add more stock or 1 cup milk while cooking.

Variation
Replace any of the dried herbs with 2 tbsp of fresh.

Variation
Add mushrooms or cauliflower to make a thicker soup.

Sweet Potato Soup with Apple and Maple Syrup

SERVES 6 TO 8

*I always remind **What's for Dinner?** viewers that a
sweet potato isn't a yam; I yam what I yam,
but I'm not a sweet "potater."*

6 cups	vegetable stock		1	small cooking onion, chopped
1 cup	apple juice		1	tbsp lemon juice
1 cup	apple sauce		1/2 tsp	dried basil
3	medium sweet potatoes, peeled and cubed (about 4 cups)		1/2 tsp	ground cinnamon
			1/2 tsp	black pepper
2	potatoes, peeled and cubed (about 1 cup)		1	bay leaf
			1/4 cup	maple syrup
2	apples, peeled, cored and cubed			

In a large soup pot, combine the stock, apple juice and apple sauce. Bring to a boil and then add the sweet potatoes, potatoes, apples, onion, lemon juice, basil, cinnamon, black pepper and bay leaf. Cook 10 minutes over medium heat to cook the sweet potatoes and the potatoes. Reduce to a simmer for another 10 minutes. Remove the bay leaf. Add maple syrup and, using a hand mixer, purée the soup to a smooth and creamy texture. Serve hot.

Cream of Cauliflower with Stilton

SERVES 4 TO 6

This is a variation on my Cauliflower and Blue Cheese Soup,
which I served to Mary Jo in our first season together;
her expression was one of bliss.

2 tbsp	olive oil	1/2 tsp	black pepper
1	medium onion, chopped	1/4 tsp	salt
6 cups	vegetable stock	2	egg yolks
1	large cauliflower, chopped	1 cup	whipping cream
1/4 cup	chopped fresh dill	1 cup	crumbled stilton cheese
1/4 cup	chopped fresh chives	2 cups	milk
1	bay leaf		

In a large, heavy saucepan, heat oil. Sauté onion in oil for 1 minute. Pour in stock and bring to a boil. Meanwhile, microwave the cauliflower, covered, at high for 1 minute. Add cauliflower to soup; reduce heat and simmer 10 minutes. Stir in half the dill, half the chives, the bay leaf, pepper and salt. Mix egg yolks with cream; stir into the soup. Mix in the stilton and milk. Simmer another 10 minutes; don't let the soup boil. Discard the bay leaf. Using a hand blender or food processor, purée the soup. Stir in the remaining dill and chives; serve immediately.

Mary Jo, could you tilt your head a little more to the left... how about a little bit more?

Butternut Soup

SERVES 4 TO 6

The butternut, a winter squash (its peak season is October through March), is my favourite gourd for soups—next to pumpkin.

Low-Fat Option
Replace the cream with low-fat milk or soy milk.

6 cups	vegetable stock	½ tsp	dried basil
3 cups	chopped butternut squash	½ tsp	dried thyme
1	medium onion, chopped	¼ tsp	ground cloves
1	medium potato, cubed	¼ tsp	nutmeg
1 tbsp	brown sugar	1	bay leaf
¾ tsp	cinnamon	1 cup	table cream
½ tsp	salt	¼ cup	chopped fresh coriander
½ tsp	black pepper		

In a large, heavy saucepan or soup pot, bring stock to a boil. Add the squash, onion, potato, brown sugar, cinnamon, salt, pepper, basil, thyme, cloves, nutmeg and bay leaf. Continue boiling until the squash and potato are tender, about 30 minutes. Discard the bay leaf. Purée the soup with a hand blender or in a food processor. Gently fold in the cream and coriander, and serve.

Pumpkin Soup with Maple Syrup

SERVES 4 TO 6

This is a great fall, winter and spring soup; it's probably the most Canadian soup we prepared during all five seasons of **What's for Dinner?**

1 tbsp	canola oil	1 cup	apple juice
1	small onion	1 cup	table cream
6 cups	vegetable stock	1/4 cup	maple syrup
3 cups	cooked pumpkin, mashed		Salt and pepper to taste
1	sweet potato, cooked and mashed	1/2 tsp	ground cinnamon
		1/4 tsp	ground nutmeg

In a large saucepan, heat oil. Sauté onion in oil for 2 to 3 minutes or until translucent. Add stock, pumpkin, sweet potato and apple juice; simmer for about 10 minutes. Add cream, maple syrup, salt and pepper; continue simmering for another 10 minutes. Before serving, add cinnamon and nutmeg.

The result of a joke not-ready-for-prime-time.

Tip
Pumpkin is one of the most abundant sources of beta-carotene.

Chicken Curry Soup with Apple and Coriander

SERVES 4 TO 6

Although you can use curry powder in this recipe, there are several excellent curry pastes in oil in most supermarkets—the oil, by the way, helps preserve their fragrance and freshness. One other thing: this soup also makes a great sauce over fettuccine or couscous.

Variation
Replace chicken with shrimp.

2 tbsp	olive oil	½ tsp	black pepper
1	medium onion, chopped	½ tsp	salt
2	cloves garlic	½ tsp	dried oregano
6 cups	chicken stock	¼ tsp	ground nutmeg
2	apples, chopped	1	bay leaf
1 cup	apple juice	2 cups	cubed cooked chicken
½ cup	white wine	½ cup	cooked rice
½ cup	frozen peas	½ cup	chopped fresh coriander
2 tbsp	mild curry powder or curry paste		

In a large skillet, heat oil. Sauté the onion and garlic for 2 to 3 minutes or until onion is translucent. Add the chicken stock, apples, apple juice, wine, peas, curry powder or paste, pepper, salt, oregano, nutmeg and bay leaf. Bring to a boil; reduce heat and simmer uncovered, stirring occasionally, for 20 minutes. If liquid reduces too much, add more apple juice. Stir in the chicken and rice; simmer another 5 minutes or until chicken is heated through. Discard bay leaf. Garnish with coriander and serve immediately.

Pamela Wallin's Smoked Salmon and Roasted Garlic Soup

SERVES 4 TO 6

*This fabulous soup is my tribute to the lovely
and talented Pamela.*

2 tbsp	olive oil		2 tbsp	chopped fresh thyme
1	large red onion, chopped		2 tbsp	chopped fresh rosemary
6	cloves garlic, chopped		1 tsp	Worcestershire sauce
2 cups	smoked salmon, chopped		1 tsp	black pepper
6 cups	vegetable stock		½ tsp	salt
½ cup	chopped fresh basil		2 cups	skim milk
¼ cup	dry sherry		½ cup	chopped fresh parsley

In a large soup pot, heat oil. Add onion, garlic and smoked salmon, and sauté for about 6 to 8 minutes. Add the stock, basil, sherry, thyme, rosemary, Worcestershire sauce, pepper and salt. Bring to a boil. Reduce to a simmer and cook for 20 minutes. Gently stir in milk and allow to simmer another 5 to 10 minutes. Serve hot, garnished with fresh parsley.

Hey Pam! I Want to be a Millionaire!

Pamela Wallin was a great guest, and a natural because she loves to cook. During her appearance, I tried to impress her by parading in my fancy shirt (which I wore especially for her). I also flashed a bit of my male charm; she was hugely unimpressed. Despite my initial setback, we had a ton of fun and, today, I consider Pamela a friend.

Cheesy Clam and Crabmeat Chowder

SERVES 4 TO 6

A chowder soup is a meal within a meal. You can add leftover vegetables—plus, use those day-old mashed potatoes.

2 tbsp	olive oil		½ cup	crabmeat
2	potatoes, diced		1 cup	table cream
1	onion, chopped		1 cup	milk
1	red pepper, chopped		½ tsp	salt
1	green pepper, chopped		1 tsp	black pepper
3 cups	vegetable stock		½ cup	grated Cheddar cheese
1 cup	clams, fresh or canned and rinsed		¼ cup	fresh dill, chopped

In a large crock pot or heavy saucepan, heat the oil. Sauté the potato and onion for 3 minutes. Add the peppers and sauté for another minute. Add the stock and bring to a boil. Reduce heat and simmer for 2 minutes. Add the clams and crabmeat; simmer for another 5 minutes. Stir in the cream, milk, salt, pepper, 1/4 cup of the Cheddar cheese and half the dill. Reduce heat and simmer for another 15 minutes, gently stirring. Make sure the soup doesn't boil. Ladle into bowls and garnish with the remaining dill and cheese.

The best of friends.

Gazpacho

SERVES 4 TO 6

*Gazpacho is a salad in a soup bowl; serve cold as a starter
with something grilled or as a whole meal with a salad.*

4 cups	vegetable broth	2	cloves garlic, chopped
2 cups	tomato juice	1 tbsp	virgin olive oil
¾ cup	chopped fresh parsley	½ tsp	black pepper
¾ cup	chopped coriander	¼ tsp	salt
2	plum tomatoes, chopped	8	jumbo shrimp, grilled and
1	green pepper, diced		sliced into pieces
1	celery stalk, chopped	¼ cup	peeled and chopped
1	small cooking onion,		seedless cucumber
	chopped		

In a blender or food processor, combine broth, tomato juice, 1/2 cup of the parsley, 1/2 cup of the coriander, tomatoes, half the green pepper, celery, onion, garlic,
olive oil, pepper and salt; blend until smooth. Strain the mixture into a bowl.
Chill, covered, in the refrigerator at least one hour prior to serving. Ladle into soup
bowls and serve, garnished with shrimp, cucumber, and the remaining green pepper, parsley and coriander.

Tips
*Add ice cubes if it
gets too warm.*

Tip
*Serve with chopped
cucumbers, tomatoes,
scallions, and other
vegetables to be tossed into
the soup to give it added
taste and texture.*

The Smart and Sassy Sidekick

A very special Christmas.

Baked Broccoli with Orange and Lemon

SERVES 6

A great holiday side—colourful and tasty.

3 cups	broccoli florets	2 tbsp	lemon rind
½ cup	orange juice	3 tbsp	orange rind
½ cup	lemon juice	½ tsp	dried tarragon or
½ cup	shredded Cheddar cheese		dried parsley

Place broccoli in a baking dish; pour the orange juice and lemon juice over the broccoli. Sprinkle with cheese, lemon rind, orange rind and tarragon; bake covered, at 350°F for about 8 to 10 minutes or until cheese is bubbling. Be careful not to overcook. Serve warm.

Poor Mary Jo!

I often played tricks on Mary Jo when the cameras were off. Sometimes, when we'd break for commercial and when she wasn't looking, I'd switch off her burners. Whatever side dish she was making would stop cooking (remember, we taped the show in real time). Don't feel too bad for her, though—she always got back at me *on camera*.

Oven-Baked Fennel and Yam

SERVES 6

Serve this flavourful side dish with fish, chicken or beef.

1 fennel bulb, cut into one-inch pieces	Vegetable oil spray
1 yam, diced	½ tsp garlic powder
1 small red onion, cut into wedges	½ tsp dried basil
2 celery stalks, sliced into one-inch pieces	½ tsp dried oregano
	½ tsp dried rosemary
	½ tsp ground black pepper

In a non-stick baking dish, combine the fennel, yam, onion and celery. Spray with vegetable oil spray for about 4 seconds. In a small bowl, combine garlic powder, basil, oregano, rosemary and black pepper; mix well. Sprinkle the mixture over the vegetables and mix well. In a preheated 350°F oven, bake the fennel for about 50 minutes or until tender, turning once.

Variation
Substitute potatoes or even turnip for the yam.

Tip
Use low-in-saturated-fat vegetable oil spray.

Grilled Eggplant with Herbs and Balsamic

SERVES 6

The eggplant (or aubergine) is delicious grilled,
and served with lamb or beef.

1	medium eggplant, sliced into circles, unpeeled	½ tsp	dried thyme
		½ tsp	garlic powder
¼ cup	balsamic vinegar	½ tsp	dried oregano
½ tsp	dried basil	½ tsp	ground black pepper

Using a kitchen brush, coat both sides of the eggplant with the balsamic vinegar. Next, combine the basil, thyme, garlic powder, oregano and black pepper in a bowl; sprinkle over both sides of the eggplant. On an outdoor or indoor grill (I like to use an indoor grill), spread the eggplant evenly and grill about 4 minutes on each side or until grill marks appear.

"Today, we're going to talk about the healthy elf."

Roasted Eggplant with Tomatoes and Fresh Basil

SERVES 6

*Add any other vegetables you wish, or have left over
in the refrigerator.*

1	small eggplant, cubed (about 2 cups)	½ cup	chopped fresh basil
2	large tomatoes, chopped	½ cup	shaved carrot
2	green peppers, chopped	2	cloves garlic, chopped
1	small red onion, chopped	½ tsp	sea salt
1 cup	chopped fresh parsley	½ tsp	black pepper
			Vegetable oil spray

Variation
*If you haven't got an
eggplant, a zucchini
will do just nicely.*

In a large salad bowl or mixing bowl, combine the eggplant, tomatoes, green peppers, onion, parsley, basil, carrot, garlic, salt and pepper. Transfer to a large baking dish; spray with vegetable oil. Bake in a preheated 350°F oven for 12 to 15 minutes, or until vegetables are tender. (Make sure the eggplant is tender, not mushy). Serve warm.

Red Wine-Glazed Carrots and Tomato

SERVES 4

*This is a lovely side dish that doubles as a thick
and delicious pasta sauce.*

1 can	(14 oz) diced stewed tomatoes	1/4 cup	red wine
1/2 cup	chopped fresh basil	1/2 tsp	sea salt
2 cups	sliced carrots	1/2 tsp	black pepper
		1/4 cup	chopped fresh parsley

In a sauté pan, heat the tomatoes and the basil together for about 2 minutes. Add the carrots, wine, salt and pepper. Simmer about 10 minutes or until carrots are tender. Garnish with fresh parsley and serve.

Getting Back at Mary Jo

Nothing was ever scripted on *What's for Dinner?* We said whatever popped into our heads—which could lead us into dangerous waters. To try to forestall disaster, we would rehearse what we would do and say during each commercial break. Of course, once the camera began to roll, I'd do and say the reverse of everything we'd worked out!

Corn and Red Pepper with Mushrooms

SERVES 6

*A most versatile side dish, this corn extravaganza
goes with just about everything.*

½ cup	vegetable stock	½ tsp	chili powder
1 cup	frozen corn	½ tsp	dried mint
1	small red pepper, chopped	1 tbsp	butter
½ cup	chopped button mushrooms		

In a saucepan, heat the stock and add the corn, red pepper, mushrooms, chili powder and dried mint. Cook for 5 minutes or until the stock has reduced by about a half. Stir in the butter and serve immediately.

Green Beans with Onion and Garlic

SERVES 4

This simple side dish is a perfect accompaniment for garlic mashed potatoes and grilled sirloin steak.

2 tbsp	butter		½ tsp	dried basil
1	clove garlic, chopped		½ tsp	black pepper
1	small onion, chopped		¼ cup	vegetable stock
½ lb	green beans			

In a medium sauté pan, melt the butter and add garlic and onion. Sauté for about 2 minutes or until onion is translucent. Add the beans, basil and black pepper; sauté for 2 minutes. Add the stock and steam the beans for about 8 minutes or until tender but not overcooked.

The end of a very long day.

Kenny's Quick & Easy Scalloped Potatoes

SERVES 4

*These scalloped potatoes are so much better than
those straight out of the box, and just as easy!*

4	medium potatoes, sliced thinly	½ tsp	dried basil
1	medium cooking onion, sliced thinly	½ tsp	garlic powder
		½ tsp	black pepper
¾ cup	table cream	1 cup	grated Cheddar cheese
		½ cup	grated Parmesan cheese

In a mixing bowl, combine the potatoes, onion, cream, basil, garlic powder and
pepper. Arrange slices in a non-stick baking dish. Bake in a preheated 350°F oven
for 20 minutes, or until the potatoes are cooked through. Add the Cheddar cheese;
top with Parmesan. Bake another 5 minutes or until the topping turns golden.

Low-Fat Options
*Replace cream with
non-fat yogurt. Replace
the Cheddar and
Parmesan with
low-fat versions.*

Curried Rice with Apples and Raisins

SERVES 4

This side dish will add some spice—
and sweetness—to any meal.

Variation
*If you don't have apples
or apple juice, cook the
rice in orange juice and
add orange rind
and mint.*

2 1/2 cups	apple juice		1/4 cup	raisins
1 cup	white rice		1/2 tsp	mild curry powder
1	medium apple, chopped and cored		1/4 tsp	cinnamon

In a medium-sized saucepan, heat the apple juice to a boil. Add the rice, apple, raisins, curry powder and cinnamon. Reduce to a simmer, and cook covered for 15 minutes. Serve immediately.

Tip
*Watch the liquid and,
if it reduces too fast,
add more apple juice
and mix.*

Asparagus Roasted in Tarragon Lemon Butter

SERVES 4

*Always-elegant asparagus gets even dressier
when napped in herbed butter.*

12	medium-sized asparagus stalks	1 tbsp	lemon rind
2 tbsp	butter	½ tsp	dried tarragon
	Juice of 1 lemon	½ tsp	salt
		½ tsp	black pepper

Trim off the rough ends of the asparagus and place stalks in foil wrap. Cover the asparagus completely with butter and lemon juice. Sprinkle with lemon rind, tarragon, salt and pepper. Seal in the foil wrap, allowing enough space inside to steam. Bake at 350°F for 8 to 10 minutes or until tender. Do not overcook.

The Vulcan Mind Meld.

Roasted Yams with Maple Syrup

SERVES 4

*Yams are a delicious variation on the more traditional
potato side dish.*

Variation
*Substitute sweet
potatoes for yams
(they're not the same
thing!).*

1 tsp	ground cinnamon		2 tbsp	apple juice concentrate
½ tsp	black pepper		1	medium apple, cored and cut into 8 wedges
¼ tsp	ground nutmeg		¼ cup	maple syrup
2	medium yams cut into wedges			

Combine the cinnamon, pepper and nutmeg in a small bowl and set aside. Place the yam wedges and apple juice concentrate in a freezer bag, and mix well so the yams become coated with the concentrate. Place the yam and apple wedges on a non-stick cookie sheet or small baking dish and sprinkle on the spice mixture. Bake uncovered in a preheated 350°F oven for 30 to 35 minutes until tender. Brush on the maple syrup and place in oven to broil for 2 minutes.

Roasted Chili Potatoes with Chives

SERVES 4

This side dish is a great accompaniment to burgers or dogs.

1 tbsp	garlic powder	4	medium potatoes, cut into cubes or wedges
1 tsp	onion powder		
½ tsp	chili powder	4	cloves garlic, peeled and cut in half
½ tsp	dried rosemary		
½ tsp	ground black pepper	¼ cup	finely chopped chives

In a bowl, combine the garlic powder, onion powder, chili powder, rosemary and pepper. Put the dry ingredient mixture in a large freezer bag and add the potato wedges; shake well to ensure even coating. Place the potatoes, garlic and chives in a non-stick oven dish. Bake uncovered at 350° for 25 minutes. Put oven on broil and broil the potatoes until golden, about 2 minutes.

Variation
Replace potatoes with yams or sweet potato.

Sautéed Pears and Apples with Blue Cheese

SERVES 4

You can serve this fabulous side dish on top of fish or grilled chicken. If you don't have pears or apples, feel free to choose any fruit you can get year-round.

Variation
Replace the fruit with other firm fruit. Replace apple juice with pear juice or cranberry juice.

2	apples, cored	½ cup	unsweetened apple juice
1	Bartlett pear, cored	½ cup	chopped fresh mint
1 tbsp	olive oil	2 tbsp	crumbled blue cheese
1	small red onion, sliced		

Cube the fruit. In a sauté pan, heat the oil and sauté the onion for about 3 minutes until translucent. Stir in the apple juice, mint, pear and apple and mix well; sauté on medium heat about 10 minutes. Add the blue cheese; sauté another minute. Can be served hot, warm or cold.

Variation
Peaches can be used, but be careful not to overcook them. Add peaches separately so they sauté only about 3 minutes.

Sautéed Spinach with Red Peppers

SERVES 6

By the fourth season of **What's for Dinner?**
*we were really cooking with great side dishes. Try this one;
it builds strength and character.*

2 tbsp	olive oil	½ cup	vegetable stock
1	medium red onion, sliced	½ tsp	salt
1	clove garlic, finely chopped	½ tsp	ground black pepper
1 lb	fresh spinach, chopped	1 tbsp	balsamic vinegar
2	red peppers, sliced		

In a wok or large deep sauté pan, heat the oil; add the onion and garlic. Cook about 2 minutes, then start to add the spinach by handfuls; the spinach will reduce, but keep mixing it in the sauté pan. Add the red peppers, stock, salt and pepper and continue to cook about 8 minutes or until liquid is reduced. Remove to a bowl or plate and sprinkle balsamic vinegar over top.

"Keep looking, Mary Jo, it's just a little to the right."

Baked Couscous with Chick-Peas and Red Wine

SERVES 6

This Middle-East influenced side dish is perfect with lamb.

Variation
Replace the couscous with 2 cups cooked rice.

1 ½ cup	vegetable stock		½ cup	red wine
1 cup	couscous		2	cloves garlic, chopped
1 cup	chopped button mushrooms		1 tsp	Dijon mustard
1 cup	canned chick-peas		½ tsp	chili powder
1 can	(14 oz) stewed tomatoes, diced		½ tsp	dried rosemary
1	small cooking onion, chopped		½ tsp	black pepper
			½ cup	chopped fresh parsley
			¼ cup	grated Parmesan cheese

In a microwave-proof dish, heat the stock until boiling; pour into a deep baking dish and add the couscous, mushrooms, chick-peas, tomatoes, onion, wine, garlic, Dijon mustard, chili powder, rosemary and pepper. Mix well and bake in an pre-heated 350°F oven for 15 minutes. Mix in the parsley and top with the Parmesan. Bake another 5 minutes or until golden.

Oven-Baked Couscous with Spinach and Fennel

SERVES 6

*Fennel with couscous? Why not?! Fennel's subtle
licorice flavour makes everything taste better!*

1 cup	couscous	1 tsp	dried parsley
2 cups	boiling water	1/2 tsp	dried tarragon
1 tbsp	olive oil	3 cups	chopped spinach
1	medium onion, diced	1/4 cup	Parmesan cheese
1	clove garlic, chopped	1/2 tsp	salt
1 can	(14 oz) stewed tomatoes	1/2 tsp	black pepper
1/2 cup	chopped fennel		

Preheat oven to 375°F. Put couscous in a medium bowl; pour in boiling water and let stand for 5 minutes. In a skillet, heat oil; sauté onions and garlic for 2 minutes or until translucent. Add tomatoes, fennel, parsley and tarragon; simmer another 5 minutes or until the liquid reduces by half. In a baking dish, combine couscous, spinach and tomato mixture; mix well. Sprinkle with Parmesan and bake, covered with foil, for 15 to 20 minutes. Remove foil, sprinkle with salt and pepper, and bake another 5 minutes before serving.

Dressing Up Rice and Risotto

Hullo, Pilgrim.

Ken's Quick Fried Rice

SERVES 4 TO 6

You can easily replace the shrimp or chicken with other types of meat, such as pork or beef; or leave out altogether and just add more vegetables.

Variations
Throw in 1 cup snow peas, or any other vegetables you have on hand. Replace garlic with 1/2 tsp chopped fresh ginger.

Low-Fat Options
Remove the skin and fat from the chicken. Instead of oil, use vegetable stock.

2 tbsp	vegetable oil		1/2 cup	chopped broccoli
1	medium onion, chopped		1/2 cup	chopped fresh parsley
2	cloves garlic, minced		2 cups	cooked rice
1	boneless chicken breast, sliced		1/4 cup	soy sauce
2	eggs, beaten		1/2 tsp	dried basil
1 cup	large shrimp		1/2 tsp	black pepper
1 cup	mushrooms, chopped		2	green onions, finely chopped
1/2 cup	bean sprouts			

In a wok or large heavy skillet, heat the oil. Quickly stir-fry the onion and garlic. Add the chicken and cook for a few minutes until just done. Push chicken to sides of wok. Scramble the eggs in the wok; push to sides. Add shrimp, mushrooms, bean sprouts, broccoli, parsley and rice; mix in chicken and eggs and stir-fry 4 to 5 minutes; do not burn. Add the soy sauce, basil and pepper; stir-fry for another 2 to 3 minutes. Garnish with green onions and serve.

Cinnamon Rice Pilaf with Nuts

SERVES 4 TO 6

A pilaf is a rice dish that hails from India and the Middle East. Briefly sautéing the spices helps them release their flavour.

2 tbsp	olive oil	1 cup	green peas
1	medium onion, chopped	4 tbsp	raisins
1/2 tsp	turmeric	3 tbsp	chopped almonds
1/2 tsp	ground ginger	3 tbsp	chopped cashews
1/2 tsp	cardamom	1 1/2	cups rice
2	cloves	1/2 tsp	cinnamon
1	bay leaf	4 cups	water
1 1/2	potatoes, diced		

In a large skillet, heat 1 tbsp of the oil. Sauté onion in oil for 3 to 4 minutes, or until lightly browned. Add turmeric, ginger, cardamom, cloves and bay leaf; sauté for less than a minute. In a different pan, heat the remaining 1 tbsp of oil. Combine potatoes, peas, raisins, almonds and cashews and sauté for 2 minutes. Add rice into the onion mixture and cook for 2 minutes while stirring. Stir in the cinnamon. Add water and bring to a boil; reduce heat and simmer until water is nearly gone, about 15 minutes. Add the vegetable and nut mixture to the rice mixture and cook covered for 5 minutes on low heat.

Curry Chicken with Peppers and Rice

SERVES 4

This is a very well balanced, hearty dinner; serve it with bruschetta, or toasted Italian bread with feta cheese and finely chopped rosemary sprinkled on top. Experiment with different types of sausages, as well as with vegetables.

Variation
Replace the chicken with large tiger shrimp.

1 tbsp	olive oil	2 cups	warmed chicken stock
1	onion, chopped	½ cup	shredded fresh spinach
2	cloves garlic, minced	1 tsp	dried tarragon
1	sweet red pepper, chopped	1 tsp	mild curry powder
1	green pepper, chopped	½ tsp	dried basil
1 cup	chopped fennel	½ tsp	salt
1 cup	sliced mushrooms	½ tsp	black pepper
1 cup	rice	2 cups	cooked, chopped chicken

In a skillet, heat the oil. Sauté onion and garlic in oil for about 2 minutes or until translucent. Add the red and green peppers, fennel, mushrooms and rice; sauté 2 minutes. Add the stock, spinach, tarragon, curry powder, basil, salt and pepper; cook 5 minutes. Pour contents into a casserole dish. Arrange the chicken on top. Bake covered, at 350°F for 15 minutes or until the rice is cooked.

2 Prima Donnas + 1 Make-Up Person = Disaster!

In year one, Mary Jo and I always used to fight for the make-up chair prior to shooting *What's for Dinner?* Whoever could, got there first—we needed as much time as possible!

Cabbage Rolls

MAKES 12 TO 16 CABBAGE ROLLS

Cabbage rolls are a part of life for some people in the prairies. My mother Helen, who was born and raised on a Saskatchewan farm, is the inspiration for this version.

1	large head green cabbage	½	sweet red pepper, finely chopped
3 cups	cooked rice	½	green pepper, finely chopped
1 cup	chopped fresh parsley		
1 cup	finely chopped celery	2	cloves garlic, minced
1	small onion, finely chopped	2	medium tomatoes, finely chopped
½ cup	grated carrot		
½ cup	chopped button mushrooms	½ tsp	salt
		1 tsp	black pepper
½ cup	fresh chopped basil	1 can	(28 oz) stewed tomatoes

In a large pot, bring 6 cups of water to boil. Core the cabbage, then blanch it in boiling water for about 4 minutes. Allow to cool and remove the leaves whole. In a medium bowl, combine the rice, parsley, celery, onion, carrot, mushrooms, 1/4 cup of the basil, red pepper, green pepper, garlic, tomatoes, salt and 1/4 tsp of the black pepper; mix well. On paper towels, lay out cabbage leaves. Spoon rice mixture into the centre of each leaf; gently fold each end and place in a casserole or baking dish. Top with stewed tomatoes, the remaining 1/4 cup of basil and the remaining ¼ tsp of black pepper. Bake at 350°F for 25 minutes.

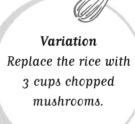

Variation
Replace the rice with 3 cups chopped mushrooms.

Variation

For a vegetarian jambalaya, replace the meat with chick-peas and the chicken stock with vegetable stock.

Low-Fat Option

Replace the olive oil with a vegetable oil such as canola, which is lower in saturated fats.

Tip

Use parboiled rice to speed up the cooking process.

Jammin' Jambalaya

SERVES 6

*A rough translation of the word **jambalaya** is "rice with a gift"; here's my gift to you.*

2 tbsp	olive oil	1 tbsp	paprika
2	chicken breasts, skinless and boneless, chopped	1 tsp	dried basil
1	mild-to-hot sausage, sliced	½ tsp	dried thyme
1	onion, diced	½ tsp	cayenne pepper
½ cup	diced celery	½ tsp	salt
½	green pepper, chopped	½ tsp	black pepper
1	clove garlic, chopped	1	bay leaf
3 cups	chicken stock	2 ½ cups	long-grain rice
1 cup	dry white wine	10	large shrimp
2	medium tomatoes, chopped	½ cup	chopped green onion

In a large skillet or crock pot, heat oil. Sauté chicken and sausage in hot oil until chicken is almost cooked; remove chicken pieces and sausage from skillet. Heat oil again; add onion, celery, green pepper and garlic; sauté for 2 to 3 minutes or until onion is translucent. Add stock, wine, tomatoes, paprika, basil, thyme, cayenne, salt, pepper and bay leaf, and bring to a boil. Stir in rice. Reduce heat and simmer for 15 minutes. Add shrimp, chicken and sausage. Mix in green onion and cook another 8 to 10 minutes, or until rice is cooked and liquid is reduced.

Paella with a Punch

SERVES 6

This stove-top paella is a meal in itself. Serve with
a jug of Sangria or a bottle of dry red wine.

4 lb	bacon, sliced		½	green pepper, chopped
2 tbsp	olive oil		4 cups	boiling water
2	chicken breasts, sliced		2 cups	rice
2	hot Italian sausages, sliced		½ cup	chopped fresh parsley
2	medium tomatoes, chopped		1 ½ tsp	black pepper
2	celery stalks, chopped		½ tsp	salt
2	cloves garlic, minced		1	bay leaf
1	small red onion, chopped		½ tsp	red pepper flakes
½	sweet red pepper, chopped		6	jumbo shrimp, peeled and deveined

Low-Fat Option
*Omit the bacon and
sausage, and sauté
in vegetable stock
instead of oil.*

In a large pot, cook bacon. Remove and drain fat. In the same pot, heat 1 tbsp of the oil. Sauté chicken and sausage in oil until they are no longer pink. Remove from pot and set aside. To the pot, add the remaining tbsp oil and heat. Add tomatoes, celery, garlic, onion, red pepper and green pepper; sauté until vegetables are tender. Stir in boiling water, rice, parsley, pepper, salt, bay leaf and red pepper flakes. Allow to simmer about 15 to 20 minutes or until rice is cooked. Five minutes before the paella is finished cooking, add the shrimp, bacon, chicken and sausage.

Stove-top Shrimp and Scallop Paella

SERVES 4 TO 6

*This is paella made simple—cook this exotic specialty
right on the top of the stove!*

4 cups	vegetable stock	1 can	(28 oz) crushed stewed tomatoes
2	cloves garlic, chopped	½ tsp	dried basil
2	celery stalks, chopped	½ tsp	dried thyme
1	medium carrot, chopped	½ tsp	chili powder
1	small onion, chopped	½ tsp	black pepper
½ cup	white wine	½ tsp	sea salt
¼ tsp	saffron	6	large shrimp, cleaned and deveined
2 cups	white rice		
1	small red pepper, chopped	6	medium scallops
1 small	green pepper, chopped		

Mr. DeMille, I'm ready for my close-up.

In a deep sauté pan or soup pot, heat 1/4 cup of the vegetable stock; sauté garlic, celery, carrot and onion in the stock about 3 to 4 minutes or until vegetables are tender. Add the remaining stock, white wine and saffron. Bring to a boil. Add the rice, red pepper, green pepper, tomatoes, basil, thyme, chili powder, black pepper and salt. Reduce heat to low and simmer for 10 minutes. Add the shrimp and scallops; cook until the rice is done, about 10 minutes.

Vegetarian Paella

SERVES 6 TO 8

*Traditional Spanish paella is made with chicken, sausage
and seafood: this version, just as tasty,
is for all my vegetarian viewers.*

1 tsp	olive oil		½ tsp	dried basil
½ cup	chopped onion		½ tsp	dried oregano
2	cloves garlic, chopped		½ tsp	black pepper
1	red pepper, chopped		½ tsp	sea salt
½ cup	finely chopped fennel		1 cup	rice
4 cups	vegetable stock		1	medium tomato, chopped
½ cup	white wine		1	small zucchini, chopped
1 tsp	chili powder		1 cup	finely chopped mushrooms

Variation
*Replace the stock with
apple juice, and add
2 cored and chopped
apples for a delicious,
spicy fruit
flavour.*

In a large soup pot or sauté pan, heat oil. Sauté onion and garlic in oil for 2 to 3 minutes or until onion is translucent. Add the red pepper and fennel; sauté another 4 minutes or until vegetables are tender. Add stock, wine, chili powder, basil, oregano, black pepper and salt. Bring to a boil and then stir in rice, tomato, zucchini and mushrooms. Mix well and reduce to a simmer. Cover and cook another 15 minutes or until rice has fluffed. Serve immediately.

Herbed Mushroom Risotto

SERVES 4

Three kinds of mushrooms makes this a great luncheon
main dish or the perfect first course for a dinner party.

5 cups	vegetable stock		½ cup	white wine
1 tbsp	olive oil		1 tsp	dried rosemary
1	small onion, chopped		1 tsp	dried thyme
2	cloves garlic, chopped		½ tsp	chili powder
2 cups	arborio rice		1	bay leaf
1 cup	sliced button mushrooms		½ tsp	black pepper
1 cup	sliced Portobello		½ tsp	sea salt
	mushrooms		1 tbsp	butter
1 cup	sliced shiitake mushrooms			

In a large pot, bring the stock to a boil; reduce to simmer. In a large, deep saucepan, heat the olive oil and gently sauté the onion and garlic for 2 or 3 minutes or until translucent. Add the rice and sauté, stirring, for another 2 minutes. Add all three types of mushrooms and mix well; sautéing for another 2 minutes. Using a ladle, add enough hot stock to just cover the rice. Cook, stirring, until stock is absorbed, approximately 10 minutes. Add the wine, rosemary, thyme, chili powder, bay leaf, pepper and salt; mix well, continuing to add hot stock, one ladle at a time; let the stock absorb before adding more. When the risotto becomes moist and creamy, remove the bay leaf and stir in the butter. Serve immediately.

Low-Fat Option
Omit the butter; use 2 tbsp vegetable stock instead of olive oil to sauté the onion, garlic and rice.

Asparagus Risotto with Mascarpone

SERVES 4

*Mascarpone is a wonderfully light and sweet Italian cheese
that is often used in desserts. Its inclusion in this
asparagus risotto makes it even more creamy and delicious.*

5 cups	chicken stock	12 to 14	asparagus spears, cleaned, with ends removed
2 tbsp	butter		
1 tbsp	oil	1/2 cup	mascarpone cheese
1	medium onion, finely chopped	1/2 cup	grated Parmesan cheese
		1/2 cup	chopped fresh basil
2 cups	arborio rice	1/2 tsp	sea salt
1 cup	white wine	1/2 tsp	black pepper

In a large pot, bring the stock to a boil; reduce to simmer. In a large, deep saucepan, melt butter and heat oil together; gently sauté the onion in butter and oil for 2 to 3 minutes or until onion is translucent. Add the rice and sauté, stirring, for about 2 minutes. Add wine and stir until it is absorbed. Using a ladle, add enough hot stock to just cover the rice. Cook, stirring, until stock is absorbed, approximately 10 minutes. Meanwhile, in a separate deep pot, blanch the asparagus in boiling water for 3 to 4 minutes; strain and rinse under cold water. Cut into half-inch pieces and set aside. To the risotto, add the mascarpone, Parmesan, basil, salt and pepper; mix well, continuing to add hot stock, one ladle at a time. Let the stock absorb before adding more. When the risotto becomes moist and creamy, stir in the asparagus, remove from heat, sprinkle with more Parmesan and serve immediately.

Chicken and White Wine Risotto

SERVES 4 TO 6

This is one of my favourite risottos: use leftover chicken.

5 cups	vegetable stock		1	red pepper, chopped
2 tbsp	olive oil		½ cup	chopped fresh basil
1	medium onion, chopped		1	bay leaf
2	cloves garlic, chopped		1 tsp	black pepper
2 cups	arborio rice		½ tsp	salt
1 cup	dry white wine		½ tsp	dried sage
2	chicken breasts, cooked and chopped into pieces		¾ cup	grated Parmesan cheese
			¼ cup	35% cream
½ cup	chopped carrots		2 tbsp	butter
2	celery stalks			

In a large pot, bring the stock to a boil; reduce to simmer. In a large, deep saucepan, heat oil; gently sauté the onion and garlic for 2 to 3 minutes or until onion is translucent. Add the rice and sauté, stirring, for about 2 minutes. Add wine and stir until it is absorbed. Using a ladle, add enough hot stock to just cover the rice. Cook, stirring, until stock is absorbed, approximately 10 minutes. Add the chicken, carrots, celery, red pepper, basil, bay leaf, pepper, salt, and sage. Mix well, continuing to add soup stock, one ladle at a time; let the stock absorb before adding more. When the risotto becomes moist and creamy, remove the bay leaf and add the Parmesan, cream and butter. Mix well and serve immediately.

Shrimp Risotto

SERVES 4

The fresh dill is the pièce-de-résistence in this delicious risotto dish.

6 cups	fish stock		Pinch of powdered saffron
2 tbsp	oil	10	large shrimp, cleaned and deveined
1	small red onion, chopped		
1	clove garlic, chopped	½ cup	grated Parmesan cheese
1 cup	arborio rice	½ cup	35% cream
1	small red pepper, chopped	2 tbsp	butter
½ cup	chopped fresh parsley	½ tsp	salt
¼ cup	chopped fresh dill	½ tsp	black pepper
¼ tsp	dried sage		

In a large pot, bring the stock to a boil; reduce to simmer. In a large, deep saucepan, heat oil; gently sauté the onion and garlic for 2 to 3 minutes or until onion is translucent. Add the rice and sauté, stirring, about 2 minutes. Using a ladle, add enough hot stock to just cover the rice. Cook, stirring, until stock is absorbed, approximately 10 minutes. Add the red pepper, parsley, dill and sage; stir well. In a ladle of stock, dilute the saffron before adding to the risotto. Mix well, continuing to add hot stock, one ladle at a time; let the stock absorb before adding more. Once all stock is absorbed, add the shrimp and continue cooking another 5 minutes, or until shrimp is cooked. When the risotto becomes moist and creamy, add the Parmesan, cream, butter, salt and pepper. Mix well and simmer for 2 minutes. Serve immediately.

Variations
Replace the shrimp with 12 medium scallops.

Variation
For a vegetarian dish, substitute 2 cups chopped mushrooms for the shrimp, and use vegetable stock instead of fish stock.

Low-Fat Options
Replace cream with low- or non-fat yogurt. Replace butter with light margarine and use low-fat Parmesan cheese.

The Pasta Diet Starts Here!

Macaroni with Cheese and Ground Beef

SERVES 6

Ground beef and macaroni with cheese is a classic of good home cooking; my version calls for a healthy dose of olive oil and low-sodium/low-fat beef stock.

Variation
Replace ground beef with ground chicken or turkey, and the stock with chicken stock. Substitute yogurt for the sour cream.

Low-Fat Option
Use low-fat or non-fat sour cream and cheese.

2 tbsp	olive oil	½ tsp	dried basil
1	medium onion, chopped	½ tsp	dried thyme
2	cloves garlic, chopped	½ tsp	dried sage
1	medium red pepper, diced	½ tsp	dried black pepper
1	lb lean ground beef	½ cup	sour cream
4 cups	low sodium/low-fat beef stock	½ cup	grated Cheddar cheese
3 cups	elbow macaroni	½ cup	fresh parsley, chopped
2	medium tomatoes, chopped		

Using a large deep sauté pan, heat the oil and sauté the onion, garlic and red pepper for about 2 minutes. Crumble in the ground beef and sauté about 10 minutes or until cooked thoroughly. Heat the stock on the stove or in the microwave oven. To the ground beef mixture, add the hot stock, macaroni, tomatoes, basil, thyme, sage and black pepper. Simmer about 10 minutes or until stock has reduced and macaroni is cooked. Mix in the sour cream and cheese and cook over low heat for another 5 minutes, continuing to stir until creamy. Mix in parsley and serve.

Fettuccine with Chicken and Mushrooms in Gorgonzola Cream Sauce

SERVES 4

When married with pasta, gorgonzola becomes the queen of cheeses; all others bow (curtsey!) down before her.

10 oz	fettuccine		1 tbsp	chopped fresh thyme
2 tbsp	olive oil		1 tbsp	chopped fresh basil
2	boneless, skinless chicken breasts, sliced		1 tsp	Worcestershire sauce
1	small red onion, chopped		1 tsp	black pepper
1 cup	chopped mushrooms		1 tsp	salt
¼ cup	white wine		1 cup	table cream
			¾ cup	gorgonzola cheese

In a large pot, cook fettuccine in 4 cups boiling water for about 7 minutes, occasionally stirring to prevent sticking. Meanwhile, in a large sauté pan, heat the oil and brown chicken for 4 to 5 minutes. Add onion and sauté about 2 minutes, or until onion is translucent. Add mushrooms, wine, thyme, basil, Worcestershire sauce, pepper and salt; cook until reduced by half. Add cream and gently stir in cheese. Stir gently for about 3 minutes or until smooth and creamy. Pour sauce on the cooked fettuccine and serve immediately.

Variation
If you're looking for a vegetarian dish, replace the chicken with another 1 1/2 cup chopped mushrooms.

Low-Fat Option
Replace cream with non-fat sour cream or yogurt.

Seafood Spaghetti with Fresh Coriander and Ginger

SERVES 6

A variation of this dish was served on our New Year's Eve show in the third season. Serve this with elegant appetizers and champagne!

Variation

If you're feeling light of purse or pocket, replace the swordfish with tuna, and the mussels or scallops with more clams.

½ tbsp	olive oil	½ tsp	black pepper
1	medium onion, chopped	¼ tsp	salt
2	cloves garlic, minced		Pinch of saffron
2 tbsp	grated fresh ginger	8	jumbo shrimp, cleaned
½ large	swordfish steak, cubed		and deveined
1 can	(14 oz) clams, rinsed	½ lb	large scallops
	and drained	½ lb	fresh mussels, cleaned
1 cup	chopped fresh coriander		and de-bearded
1 cup	fish stock	2 cups	cooked spaghetti
½ cup	white wine	½ cup	freshly grated
½ cup	chopped fresh parsley		Parmesan cheese

In a large saucepan, heat oil; sauté onion, garlic and ginger 2 to 3 minutes or until onion is translucent. Add the swordfish and sauté gently for about 2 minutes. Add clams, coriander, fish stock, white wine, 1/4 cup of the parsley, salt, pepper and saffron. Simmer over low heat approximately 10 to 15 minutes. Add shrimps, scallops and mussels; cook for 5 minutes or until the mussel shells have opened (be sure to discard any that don't open). Add the cooked spaghetti and mix well. Place in a large serving dish. Garnish with the remaining 1/4 cup of parsley and the Parmesan cheese.

Bow Ties with Fresh Herbs, Mushrooms and Tomatoes

SERVES 6

This fifth-season recipe proved a winner with viewers.
They keep cajoling me to give them the recipe...so, here it is!

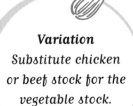

Variation
Substitute chicken or beef stock for the vegetable stock.

2 tbsp	olive oil
1	medium onion, chopped, or 4 shallots, chopped
2 cups	chopped button mushrooms
1 can	(14 oz) stewed tomatoes, drained and chopped
½ cup	chopped fresh basil or ½ tsp dried basil
¼ cup	chopped fresh oregano
¼ cup	chopped fresh sage
½ cup	vegetable stock
3 cups	bow tie pasta
¼ cup	chopped fresh parsley

In a large sauté pan, heat the oil and sauté the onion or shallots 2 to 3 minutes or until translucent. Add the mushrooms, tomatoes, basil, oregano and sage; sauté another 2 to 3 minutes. Stir in the stock and simmer 12 to 15 minutes or until liquid has reduced by half. While sauce is cooking, prepare the pasta by boiling in 5 cups salted water for 8 to 10 minutes or until tender; drain, rinse and set aside. Add the cooked pasta to the reduced sauce and mix well. Garnish with fresh parsley and serve immediately.

Rotini with Zucchini and Parmesan

SERVES 6

From season four, this one-dish wonder needs
no introduction, or sidekick!

Low-Fat Option
Instead of olive oil,
sauté in low-fat vegetable
stock. Use low-fat
Parmesan instead of
regular cheese.

Low-Fat Option
Replace table cream
with non-fat or
low-fat yogurt or
sour cream.

2 tbsp	olive oil	1 tbsp	chopped fresh thyme
1	small onion, chopped	½ tsp	sea salt
1	small sweet red pepper, sliced	½ tsp	ground black pepper
2	cloves garlic, chopped	3 cups	rotini pasta
⅔ cups	vegetable stock	½ cup	table cream
½ cup	chopped fresh basil	1	medium zucchini, cubed
2 tbsp	chopped fresh sage	½ cup	freshly grated Parmesan cheese

In a large sauté pan, heat olive oil and gently sauté the onion, red pepper and garlic for 2 to 3 minutes or until onion is translucent. Add the stock, basil, sage, thyme, salt and pepper. Allow to simmer another 5 minutes or until liquid has reduced by half. Meanwhile, in a large stock pot, boil 6 cups of salted water and cook the rotini for about 7 minutes or until tender. Drain, rinse with cold water and set aside. Reduce heat under the sauce, and mix in the cream until smooth. Add the zucchini and simmer about 5 minutes. Stir in the Parmesan cheese and the cooked rotini. Mix and serve.

Spaghetti with Roasted Vegetables

SERVES 6

*This is a great recipe for left-over grilled vegetables;
prepare it the day after your barbecue backyard party.*

1 cup	grilled mushrooms, chopped	½ tsp	dried oregano
1	onion, quartered and roasted	½ tsp	paprika
		½ lb	spaghetti
1	small roasted sweet red pepper, sliced	½ cup	vegetable stock
		¼ cup	apple juice
1	small roasted green pepper, sliced	½ tsp	dried basil
		½ tsp	sea salt
½ cup	cubed, roasted zucchini	½ tsp	black pepper
½ cup	roasted broccoli florets	½ cup	chopped fresh parsley
1 tsp	garlic powder	¼ cup	freshly grated Parmesan cheese
½ tsp	dried rosemary		

Variation
*Replace vegetables
in the recipe with
any you have or
prefer.*

In a large mixing bowl, combine the mushrooms, onion, red pepper, green pepper, zucchini and broccoli. In a small mixing bowl, combine the garlic powder, rosemary, oregano and paprika; toss well. Mix spices into the vegetables. Place vegetables on a non-stick cooking pan and set aside. Meanwhile, in a large stock pot, cook spaghetti in 6 cups boiling, salted water for about 8 to 10 minutes or until tender; drain, rinse with water and set aside. Set oven to broil and place in pan of vegetables; broil about 5 minutes and turn. Broil another 2 minutes, remove and roughly chop. In a large saucepan, heat stock, apple juice, basil, salt and pepper. Add the roasted vegetables, cooked pasta and parsley. Heat another 2 minutes, add Parmesan cheese, mix well and serve.

Penne with Blue Cheese and Spinach

SERVES 4

The blue cheese and cream combine to make the smoothest,
most velvety pasta sauce you've ever tasted!

1 tbsp	olive oil		½ tsp	dried oregano
2 cups	chopped spinach		½ tsp	dried basil
1	small onion, chopped		½ tsp	salt
2	cloves garlic, minced		½ tsp	black pepper
¼ cup	chopped fresh parsley		4 cups	penne
¼ cup	dry white wine		¼ cup	table cream
½ tsp	dried rosemary		½ cup	blue cheese

In a large sauté pan, heat the oil. Sauté spinach, onion, garlic and parsley 2 to 3 minutes or until onion is translucent. Add the wine, rosemary, oregano, basil, salt and pepper; simmer for about 5 minutes. Meanwhile, in a large stockpot, cook the penne in 6 cups boiling salted water for about 8 to 10 minutes or until tender. Drain, rinse and set aside. Add cream to sauce in saucepan; mix well for another 5 minutes, allowing liquid to reduce to half. Stir in the blue cheese, stirring gently, until sauce is smooth and creamy. Add the penne to the sauce and mix well. Serve immediately.

Beauty and the Beast.

Grilled Portobello Mushrooms over Penne

Meaty portobellos make this a satisfying main dish.

3 cups	penne	1 cup	table cream
2	large portobello mushrooms	½ cup	white wine
1 tbsp	vegetable oil	½ tsp	dried basil
½ tsp	salt	½ tsp	dried thyme
½ tsp	black pepper	½ cup	chopped fresh Italian parsley
2 tbsp	butter	¼ cup	grated Parmesan cheese
2	cloves garlic, minced		
½ cup	chopped button mushrooms		

In a large pot, bring 6 cups water to a boil. Cook penne for 8 to 10 minutes or until tender. Drain, rinse and set aside. Using a paper towel, gently clean the tops of the portobello mushrooms; brush them with vegetable oil. Sprinkle portobellos with salt and pepper, and let sit about 2 minutes before grilling. Grill the bottoms first, about 2 minutes. Turn over and grill about 5 minutes or until grill marks appear; remove and set aside. In a large frying pan or wok, melt butter. Sauté garlic and button mushrooms in butter for 2 to 3 minutes. Stir in cream, wine, basil and thyme; simmer 10 to 12 minutes or until liquid has reduced by half. Add penne and mix well. Top with sliced portobello mushrooms and parsley. Sprinkle with Parmesan and serve.

Penne with Beef Tenderloin and Fresh Basil

SERVES 6

*If I remember it correctly, in the fourth-season show
featuring this pasta delight, Mary Jo got snippy with the beef
and I got fresh with the basil!*

Variation
*To make this a vegetarian
dish, replace the beef with
4 portobello mushrooms
and use vegetable
stock instead of
beef stock.*

2 tbsp	olive oil
1	small red onion, sliced
2	cloves garlic, chopped
2 6-oz	tenderloin steaks, sliced
3 cups	penne
2	large tomatoes, chopped
½ cup	chopped fresh basil or 1 tsp dried basil

¼ cup	beef stock
¼ cup	red wine
½ cup	chopped fresh parsley
½ tsp	sea salt
½ tsp	black pepper

In a large sauté pan, heat the oil. Sauté onion 2 to 3 minutes or until translucent. Add the garlic and sauté another minute; add the steak and sauté 4 minutes. Meanwhile, in a large stockpot, cook the penne in 6 cups boiling salted water for 8 to 10 minutes or until tender. Drain, rinse and set aside. To the saucepan, add the tomatoes, basil, stock, red wine, parsley, salt and pepper; cook stirring for another 5 minutes, allowing liquid to reduce by half. Add the penne to the sauce and mix well. Serve immediately.

BEST OF WHAT'S FOR DINNER?

Penne with Turkey Sausage and Sweet Red Pepper in a Creamy Tomato Sauce

SERVES 4

Turkey sausage is a delicious alternative
to other types of sausages.

2 tbsp	olive oil	½ cup	red wine
2	large turkey sausages	½ tsp	dried basil
1	small cooking onion, chopped	½ tsp	dried mint
		½ tsp	paprika
2	cloves garlic, chopped	½ tsp	salt
1 can	(14 oz) stewed tomatoes, drained and chopped	1 tsp	black pepper
		½ cup	cream
2	medium sweet red peppers, diced	2 cups	penne

In a large sauté pan, heat oil. Add turkey sausages and cook through. Remove, slice into 1-inch pieces, and set aside. In the pan, sauté onion and garlic 2 to 3 minutes or until the onion is translucent. Add tomatoes, red peppers, red wine, basil, mint, paprika, salt and pepper. Reduce heat and allow mixture to simmer about 5 to 8 minutes. Add cream and gently stir. Meanwhile, in a large stockpot, cook penne in 6 cups of slightly salted water for about 8 to 10 minutes or until tender. Drain and rinse with cold water. Add penne and sausage to the sauce in the pan. Mix well and serve immediately.

Variation
Substitute either chicken or beef sausage for the turkey sausage.

Low-Fat Option
Replace cream with non-fat sour cream.

Fusilli with Ham and Mushrooms in a Basil Cream Sauce

SERVES 4 TO 6

The hint of sherry makes this cream sauce extra luxurious.

3 cups	fusilli		¾ cup	table cream
2 tbsp	butter		½ cup	chopped fresh parsley
1	small onion, chopped		½ cup	chopped fresh basil
2	cloves garlic, minced			Salt and pepper to taste
1 cup	sliced mushrooms		½ cup	grated Parmesan cheese
1 tbsp	sherry			
8	slices cooked ham, cut into strips			

In a large stockpot, cook the fusilli in 6 cups boiling salted water for about 8 to 10 minutes or until tender. Drain, rinse with cold water, and set aside. To prepare the sauce, heat the butter in a large sauté pan. Sauté onion and garlic 2 to 3 minutes or until onion is translucent. Add the mushrooms and cook, stirring constantly, for 5 minutes or until mushrooms are tender. Pour in sherry and allow to burn off. Add the ham, cream, parsley, basil, salt and pepper. Sauté about 5 minutes or until sauce thickens. Add Parmesan and fusilli and mix well; serve immediately.

If I Had a Million Dollars . . .

The Barenaked Ladies actually launched a new album on the show! It was a big moment, but these guys are really down to earth. It's so nice to see guys like these, who've made it so big, remain nice and unaffected by all the adulation.

"Pssst, Mary Jo, your trap door's wiiide open!"

Fusilli with Goat Cheese

SERVES 6

This is delicious as is, but feel free to substitute low-fat cream cheese for the cheese, and vegetable stock for the wine to make a low-fat treat.

3 tbsp	olive oil
1	small cooking onion, chopped
2	cloves garlic, chopped
½ cup	mushrooms, chopped
1	small red pepper, chopped
½ cup	white wine
2 tbsp	chopped fresh basil, or ½ tsp dried basil
1 tbsp	chopped fresh oregano, or ¼ tsp dried oregano
½ tsp	sea salt
½ tsp	ground black pepper
3 cups	fusilli
¾ cup	mild soft goat cheese

Whistler's mother.

In a sauté pan, heat the oil. Sauté the onion for 2 to 3 minutes or until translucent. Add the garlic, mushrooms and red pepper; cook another 3 minutes. Add the wine, basil, oregano, salt and pepper; cook another 2 minutes. Meanwhile, in a large stockpot, cook fusilli in 6 cups of boiling salted water for about 8 to 10 minutes or until tender. Drain, rinse and set aside. In the sauté pan, stir in the goat cheese and mix until smooth. Add the pasta and mix well. Serve immediately.

Pasta Primavera

SERVES 4

Pasta primavera is a perennial favourite. The jalapeños
and red wine give this version a zippy kick.

3 tbsp	olive oil	½ cup	chopped black olives
1	small onion, chopped	½ cup	red wine
2	cloves garlic, minced	2 tbsp	apple juice concentrate or
1 can	(14 oz) stewed tomatoes		1 tbsp brown sugar
1	small sweet red pepper, diced	½ tsp	chopped jalapeño peppers
		½ tsp	dried oregano
1	small sweet green pepper, diced	½ tsp	salt
		½ tsp	black pepper
½ cup	diced zucchini	1	bay leaf
½ cup	diced carrots	2 cups	fusilli pasta
½ cup	chopped fresh basil		

In a large sauté pan, heat oil. Sauté onion and garlic in oil 2 to 4 minutes or until onion is translucent. Add tomatoes, red pepper, green pepper, zucchini, carrots, basil, olives, wine, apple juice or sugar, jalapeños, oregano, salt, pepper and bay leaf; simmer for 15 to 20 minutes or until liquid is reduced by half and sauce has thickened. Meanwhile, in a large stockpot, cook fusilli in 6 cups of boiling salted water for about 8 to 10 minutes or until tender. Drain and rinse. Add fusilli to pan, mix well and serve.

Oriental Noodles with Bacon

SERVES 4 TO 6

*Cooking in a wok is a wonderfully efficient way
to prepare food. This recipe packs maximum flavour
into minimum cooking time.*

1 pkg	rice vermicelli noodles (makes about 2 cups)	2	onions, sliced
3	eggs	1	sweet red pepper, sliced into strips
2	large carrots, thinly sliced	1/4 cup	soy sauce
1 lb	bacon, chopped	2 tbsp	oyster sauce
3 cups	bean sprouts		Black pepper to taste
2	cloves garlic, minced	1/2 cup	chopped green onions

In a large bowl, soak noodles in cold water until soft and fluffy, about 30 minutes; drain. In a medium bowl, beat eggs; pour into a heated, greased frying pan. Fry eggs until set on the bottom; turn and fry other side until cooked thoroughly. Remove and let cool; slice into thin strips. In a large wok, bring 1/2 cup water to a boil. Place carrots in a steamer in the wok and steam covered for 3 to 5 minutes or until tender; remove carrots from wok and discard water. Place bacon in the wok and cook until almost crispy. Reduce heat and mix in bean sprouts, garlic, onions and red pepper, stir-frying for 4 minutes or until onions are translucent. Mix in noodles, soy sauce, oyster sauce, carrots and eggs; continue stir-frying until heated through. Add pepper to taste. Spoon stir-fry into a platter, or large bowl, and top with green onions. Serve immediately.

Low-Fat Option
Replace bacon with a low-fat turkey bacon.

Grilled Shrimp in a Red Pepper Cream Sauce over Egg Noodles

SERVES 4 TO 6

Red peppers can also be referred to as capsicums,
which comes from the Latin word for "case."
This recipe is divine—case closed!

Variations
Replace shrimp with squid or other grilled firm fish. Replace pasta with leftover rice.

12	jumbo shrimp, peeled and deveined	½ cup	red wine
	Salt and pepper	¼ cup	chopped fresh basil
1 tbsp	butter	2 tbsp	chopped fresh thyme
4	shallots, chopped	2 tbsp	chopped fresh oregano
2	cloves garlic, chopped	¼ cup	chopped fresh Italian parsley
1	sweet red pepper, finely chopped	½ cup	table cream
		3 cups	cooked egg noodles

Skewer the shrimp, place on a paper towel and sprinkle each side with salt and pepper. Let sit for about two minutes. Heat the grill; place skewers on and grill each side for 2 minutes or until sear marks appear. Remove shrimp and set aside. Meanwhile, in a large skillet, melt butter. Sauté shallots and garlic in butter for 1 minute. Add the red pepper and sauté until tender. Mix in the wine, basil, thyme, oregano and half the parsley; let liquid reduce to half and then gently stir in cream. Continue stirring until sauce has a creamy texture. Spoon the sauce onto the egg noodles and arrange the skewered shrimp on top. Sprinkle with remaining parsley and serve.

Linguini with Jumbo Shrimp

SERVES 4

*This first-season pasta entrée has always garnered
a lot of mail requests: here it is again. Enjoy!*

3 tbsp	olive oil	1 tbsp	lemon juice
3	cloves garlic, chopped	1 tsp	paprika
1	large sweet red pepper, sliced into strips	½ tsp	hot sauce
10	jumbo shrimp, peeled and deveined	½ tsp	salt
½ cup	chopped fresh parsley	½ tsp	black pepper
¼ cup	apple juice	2	handfuls linguini
4	green onions, sliced diagonally	½ cup	freshly grated Parmesan cheese

In a large skillet, sauté the garlic in 2 tbsp of the oil for 1 minute. Add the red pepper and the shrimp; sauté, turning constantly, until the shrimp turn white. Remove from skillet and set aside. To the skillet add the remaining olive oil, 1/4 cup of the parsley, the apple juice, green onions, lemon juice, paprika, hot sauce, salt and pepper. Simmer, allowing some of the liquid to cook away. Meanwhile, in a large pot of boiling water, cook linguini until tender but firm; drain and place on plates. Spoon sauce onto the linguini and arrange the shrimp on top. Sprinkle with remaining parsley and the Parmesan cheese.

Mixed Seafood Rigatoni with Plum Tomatoes

SERVES 4 TO 6

This perfect blend of pasta, fruits of the sea, fresh herbs
and tomatoes is redolent of summer.

½ tsp	dried basil	2 tbsp	olive oil
½ tsp	paprika	4	shallots, chopped
½ tsp	onion powder	2	cloves garlic, chopped
½ tsp	garlic powder	1	sweet red pepper, chopped
¼ tsp	cayenne pepper	1 cup	water
6	jumbo shrimp, cleaned	½ cup	red wine
	and deveined	1 tbsp	honey
6	jumbo scallops	1 tbsp	chopped fresh sage
1	small swordfish steak,	1 tbsp	chopped fresh mint
	cut into 2-inch cubes	1 tsp	tomato paste
4	plum tomatoes		Salt and pepper to taste
3 cups	rigatoni		

Soak four 12-inch wooden skewers in water for 10 to 15 minutes. Meanwhile, in a medium bowl, mix together the basil, paprika, onion powder, garlic powder and cayenne. Fold in the shrimps, scallops and swordfish, making sure the seafood is well-coated with the mixture. Thread the shrimp, scallops, swordfish pieces and plum tomatoes on the 4 skewers. Set aside. In a large pot, boil 6 cups of slightly salted water. Add rigatoni and continue boiling for 8 to 10 minutes or until rigatoni is tender. Remove pasta, drain and rinse with cold water; set aside. In a large sauté pan, heat the oil and sauté the shallots, garlic and red pepper for 2 minutes or until pepper is tender and the shallots are translucent. Add the water, wine, honey, sage, mint, tomato paste, salt and pepper to taste. Simmer 10 to 15 minutes or until liquid is reduced. Five minutes before the sauce is done, place the brochettes on a heated grill, and grill until seafood lightens in colour and vegetables are tender. Serve brochettes on a bed of rigatoni and spoon on sauce. Serve immediately.

Mediterranean Pasta Spanish-Style

SERVES 4

*Don't let the short list of ingredients fool you—this pasta dish
is packed with flavour. Olé!*

3 tbsp	+ 1 tsp olive oil	1 can	(14 oz) clams, rinsed and drained
2 cups	shell pasta	1 cup	chopped fresh parsley
1	small onion, chopped	½ tsp	salt
2	cloves garlic, chopped	½ tsp	black pepper
2 cups	large shrimp, peeled and deveined	½ cup	grated Parmesan cheese

To a large pot of boiling salted water, add 1 tsp of the oil. Cook pasta in water until tender but firm; drain and set aside. Meanwhile, in a large sauté pan, heat the remaining 3 tbsp oil. Sauté the onions and garlic in oil for 2 minutes—do not burn the garlic. Add the shrimp and cook for 1 minute. Add the clams, parsley, salt and pepper. Cook another 5 minutes. Add pasta and Parmesan cheese to sauce and stir well. Serve immediately.

"Weee're OFF to see the wizard..."

Squeeze Me Mama's Smoked Salmon Pasta

SERVES 2

*No **Best of What's for Dinner?** cookbook would be complete*
without this first-season, second-episode recipe, which I
borrowed from a restaurant in Rome.
This is definitely the best!

Low-Fat Option
Replace whipping cream
and table cream with
non-fat sour cream
and yogurt.

2 tbsp	butter	½ cup	35% whipping cream
1	small onion, chopped, or	½ cup	table cream
	4 shallots, chopped	1 tbsp	fresh thyme or
½ cup	finely chopped		½ tsp dried thyme
	sweet red pepper	½ tsp	salt
1	clove garlic, chopped	½ tsp	black pepper
1 cup	smoked salmon, chopped	½ cup	grated Parmesan cheese
¼ cup	red wine	1 cup	bow tie pasta

In a saucepan, melt the butter over medium heat. Sauté the onions and red pepper
for one minute. Add the garlic and sauté another minute. Add the smoked salmon
and red wine and cook 2 minutes. Stir in the two kinds of cream, thyme, salt, half
the black pepper and ¼ cup of the Parmesan cheese. Immediately reduce heat to
low. Stir gently until the mixture starts to thicken, about 5 minutes. Do not allow
mixture to boil or cream will curdle. Remove from heat and keep warm. In a large
pot of boiling salted water, cook pasta until tender but firm. Drain. Pour sauce over
pasta and toss gently. Sprinkle each serving with remaining pepper and Parmesan
cheese.

Vegetables as the Main Event

The newlyweds: not!

Tofu with Spicy Noodles in a Peanut Sauce

SERVES 4 TO 6

An Asian-inspired treat, spiced up with the
versatile jalapeño pepper.

Tip
When handling jalapeño
peppers, it's a good idea to
wear thin latex gloves.
Be careful not to touch
your face or rub
your eyes!

2 tbsp	olive oil	2 tbsp	vegetable stock
1 lb	firm tofu, sliced	2 tbsp	peanut butter
1 cup	chopped mushrooms	1 tbsp	balsamic vinegar
1	red onion, chopped	1 tsp	finely chopped
2	cloves garlic, minced		jalapeño peppers
½ tsp	minced fresh ginger	2 cups	cooked rice noodles
½ cup	soy sauce	1	sweet red pepper, chopped

In a wok or large skillet, heat the olive oil. Add the tofu, mushrooms, onion, garlic and ginger, and stir-fry 3 to 5 minutes until tender. Remove tofu and set aside. Add soy sauce, vegetable stock, peanut butter, balsamic vinegar and jalapeño peppers. Mix together. Add noodles and red pepper. Stir fry 3 to 4 minutes or until liquid is reduced by half. Return tofu to wok, mix well and serve immediately.

Tofu Stir-Fry with Orange and Mint

SERVES 4

*Try this with a side dish of white basmati rice
and steamed spinach.*

2 tsp	olive oil	1 cup	bean sprouts
2 packages	firm tofu, cubed	½ cup	orange juice
1 cup	chopped broccoli	½ tsp	black pepper
1	red onion, sliced	¼ tsp	salt
1	sweet red pepper, sliced into strips	1	small can mandarin oranges, drained
1	sweet green pepper, sliced into strips	½ cup	chopped fresh parsley
2	medium carrots, sliced	¼ cup	chopped fresh mint
½ tsp	chopped fresh ginger	2 tbsp	grated orange zest

In a wok or large skillet, heat the oil over high heat. Add the tofu and stir fry until golden at the edges. Remove tofu and set aside. Add the broccoli, onion, red pepper, green pepper, carrots and ginger; stir-fry for 5 minutes. Add the bean sprouts and stir fry for 1 to 2 minutes. Reduce heat to medium and stir in tofu, orange juice, pepper and salt; cook about 2 minutes. Stir in the mandarin oranges, parsley and mint, and cook for 1 minute. Garnish with orange zest and serve.

Tip
Be careful to use only the top, coloured layer of the orange rind, and not the bitter white pith underneath.

Tofu Stir-Fry with Tomatoes and Basil

SERVES 4 TO 6

*Try serving this simple stir-fry with a fennel and radicchio
salad with lemon vinaigrette*

1 package	firm tofu		2	cloves garlic, minced
2 tsp	paprika		1 can	(2 oz) stewed tomatoes
2 tbsp	olive oil		½ cup	shredded fresh sweet basil
1 cup	shredded purple cabbage		1 bunch	green onions, chopped
½ cup	chopped fennel		¼ cup	soy sauce
2	carrots, shredded		2 tbsp	balsamic vinegar

Cube tofu and arrange pieces on a greased cooking sheet. Sprinkle tofu with paprika and bake at 350°F for about 10 minutes. In a wok, heat the olive oil and sauté the cabbage, fennel, carrots and garlic for about 2 minutes. Add stewed tomatoes, basil, green onions, soy sauce, balsamic vinegar, and tofu. Mix well and cook about 2 minutes.

Tip

Parboiling dense vegetables before stir-frying will help get everything done at the same time.

Tip

When preparing fennel, be sure trim off and discard the stalks and fronds.

Vegetable Casserole with Tofu and Herbs

SERVES 4 TO 6

*Tofu doesn't have to be boring. Accompanied by lots
of fresh veggies and a tangy sauce, you won't want
to remember life before soy!*

2	large tomatoes, chopped	½ cup	soft tofu
1 can	(19 oz) crushed tomatoes	½ cup	vegetable stock
1 cup	cubed eggplant	¼ cup	apple juice concentrate
2	carrots, sliced on a diagonal	2 tbsp	Dijon mustard
		1 tbsp	balsamic vinegar
2	medium potatoes, cubed	1 tsp	dried thyme
2	celery stalks, chopped	1 tsp	dried basil
1	red onion, chopped	1 tsp	dried oregano
1 cup	cubed butternut squash	½ tsp	dried sage
1	green pepper, chopped	½ tsp	salt
1 lb	firm tofu, cubed	½ tsp	pepper
1	sweet red pepper, chopped	1	bay leaf
2	cloves garlic		

In a large casserole dish, combine tomatoes, eggplant, carrots, potatoes, celery, onion, squash, green pepper and firm tofu. In a blender or food processor, combine the red pepper, garlic, soft tofu, stock, apple juice concentrate, Dijon mustard, balsamic vinegar, thyme, basil, oregano, sage, salt and pepper; purée until smooth. Pour the sauce over the vegetables, add the bay leaf, and bake uncovered at 350°F for 15 to 20 minutes, checking occasionally to make sure the vegetables are not overcooking. As soon as the vegetables are tender, discard the bay leaf and serve.

Baked Tofu with Minty Green Pepper Sauce

SERVES 4 TO 6

Mint sauce isn't just for lamb anymore...

1	medium onion, chopped	1 tsp	balsamic vinegar
2	cloves garlic, minced	½ tsp	black pepper
½ cup	fresh chopped mint	½ tsp	salt
½ cup	white wine	1 bay	leaf
¼ cup	fresh chopped parsley	2	green peppers, chopped
½ bulb	fennel, chopped	1 ½	firm tofu blocks,
2 tbsp	lemon juice		cut into ½-inch strips
1 tbsp	brown sugar		

In a shallow baking dish, mix together onion, garlic, mint, wine, parsley, fennel, lemon juice, brown sugar, balsamic vinegar, pepper, salt and bay leaf. Remove 3 tbsp of the mixture and purée the remaining mixture with green pepper in a food processor. Reserve 1/2 cup of the puréed mixture for garnish. Stir remaining purée into the 3 tbsp of herb-wine mixture to make the marinade. Marinate the tofu in the baking dish for 10 to 15 minutes, turning occasionally. Bake in the oven at 350°F for 8 to 10 minutes, turning occasionally. Arrange on plate and garnish with the reserved green pepper purée.

Vegetable and Tofu Brochettes with Herbs

SERVES 6 TO 8

Grilling imparts a great smoky flavour to the tofu and veggies.

½ cup	light soy sauce or tamari		1	large zucchini, cubed
2	cloves garlic, minced		2 cups	sliced assorted mushrooms
1 tsp	olive oil		1 cup	cubed eggplant
1 tsp	dried basil		1 cup	coarsely chopped fennel
1 tsp	dried oregano		1	medium red or purple onion, cut into chunks
1 tsp	dried rosemary			
½ tsp	salt			
½ tsp	pepper			
1 lb	firm tofu, cubed			
2	sweet red or green peppers, cut into large squares			

Soak eight 8-inch wooden skewers in water for 30 minutes before using. In a large mixing bowl mix well the soy sauce, garlic, olive oil, basil, oregano, rosemary, salt and pepper. Add the tofu, peppers, zucchini, mushrooms, eggplant and fennel. Toss in mixture and coat well. Thread onion chunks, tofu and other vegetables onto skewers. Grill, turning occasionally, until grill marks are present, 5 to 8 minutes.

Why does she always have to go and do that?

Mushroom and Vegetable Kabobs with Fresh Herbs

SERVES 4 TO 6

Take advantage of the fresh herbs available during summer months to prepare this lovely grilled vegetable dish.

4 cups	chopped button mushrooms		1	red onion, chopped
2	red peppers chopped into large pieces		1 cup	chopped fresh parsley
2	zucchini, chopped into large pieces		½ cup	chopped fresh basil
1 cup	broccoli florets		½ cup	chopped fresh dill
1 cup	cauliflower florets		½ cup	lemon juice
1 cup	chopped fennel		¼ cup	chopped fresh rosemary
			¼ cup	chopped fresh oregano
			½ tsp	salt
			½ tsp	black pepper

Soak eight 8-inch wooden skewers in water for 30 minutes. Meanwhile, place mushrooms, peppers, zucchini, broccoli, cauliflower, fennel and onion in a large mixing bowl. Add parsley, basil, dill, lemon juice, rosemary, oregano, salt and pepper. Toss to coat vegetables well. Thread vegetables onto skewers and grill 5 to 10 minutes, turning occasionally to obtain grill marks.

Grilled Vegetable Kabobs with Apple and Cinnamon

SERVES 6

Apples, along with many other fruits, do very nicely on the grill. You'll love these savoury apple and vegetable kabobs.

2	large apples, cored and cubed	20	large button mushrooms
1	medium zucchini, cubed	½ bunch	broccoli, cut into florets
1	green pepper, chopped into large pieces	½ head	cauliflower, coarsely chopped
1	red pepper, chopped into large pieces	½ cup	apple juice
1	medium red onion, cut into wedges	½ tsp	dried basil
		½ tsp	dried oregano
		1 tsp	cinnamon

Soak six 8-inch wooden skewers in water for 30 minutes. Meanwhile, combine the apples, zucchini, green and red peppers, onion, mushrooms, broccoli, cauliflower and apple juice in a large mixing bowl. Sprinkle with basil, oregano and ½ tsp of the cinnamon. Mix well, then add the remaining cinnamon. Thread the vegetables and apples onto skewers and grill about 8 to 10 minutes, turning occasionally to obtain grill marks.

Variation
Sweet peppers come in an array of colours—yellow, orange, red, purple, black and salmon—that will add variety to this meal.

Grilled Portobello Mushrooms

SERVES 4

*The rich, meaty taste of the portobello mushroom,
the biggest mushroom you can buy, makes it ideal for grilling.
Serve this dish with rice or garlic mashed potatoes.*

4	large portobello mushrooms (or 8 medium)	2 tsp	Dijon mustard
2	cloves garlic, minced	1 tsp	balsamic vinegar
2 tbsp	sesame oil	1/4 tsp	thyme
2 tbsp	olive oil	1 tbsp	roasted sesame seeds, for garnish
2 tbsp	light soy sauce		

Using a damp cloth, clean the tops of the mushrooms. In a bowl, combine the garlic, sesame oil, olive oil, soy sauce, Dijon mustard, balsamic vinegar and thyme. Gently brush the mixture over the mushrooms. Grill the mushrooms for about 2 minutes on each side, or until grill marks appear. Garnish with roasted sesame seeds.

> **Tip**
> Don't soak portobello mushrooms in water, as they are porous and will retain too much liquid.

Fashion Faux-Pas

I really gave Mary Jo a hard time about her appearance and wardrobe. Whenever we were just about to go on air, I'd turn to her and say, with a look of dismay, "You're not going to wear *that* on national television, are you?!" Once the cameras started, however, I'd turn to her and exclaim, "Mary Jo, I've got to tell you, you look absolutely beautiful today in that outfit!" Mary Jo, who gives as good as she gets, would smile sweetly and remark, "Well, I'm not surprised you like it, since *you* wore it yesterday."

Stuffed Zucchini with Mushrooms

SERVES 6

*Serve this dish hot or cold, as a main course or
as a small salad.*

3	large zucchinis	1	celery stalk, chopped
2 tbsp	olive oil	½ cup	chopped fennel
1	small cooking onion, chopped	½ cup	chopped fresh parsley or ½ tsp dried parsley
2	cloves garlic, minced	½	red sweet pepper, chopped
1 cup	chopped button mushrooms	1 tbsp	lemon juice
1	small carrot, shredded	½ tsp	black pepper
		½ tsp	sea salt

Cut off the ends of the zucchini and cut them into 3-inch rounds. Scoop out the centre of each piece, creating a cup shape or barrel. In a sauté pan, heat the oil and sauté the onion and garlic for about 2 minutes over medium heat. Add the mushrooms, carrot, celery, fennel, parsley, red pepper, lemon juice, salt and pepper. Sauté about 4 minutes. Evenly stuff each zucchini with the mixture and place on a baking pan; bake at 350°F for about 15 minutes. Serve hot or cold.

Tip
Zucchini is a good source of beta-carotene, an important cancer-fighting phytochemical.

Stir-Fried Noodles and Vegetables with Curry

SERVES 4

*Cooked too much pasta? This is a great way to use it up,
as well as those veggies hanging out in the fridge.*

2 tbsp	olive oil	½ cup	halved snow peas
1 tsp	sesame oil	2 cups	cooked spaghetti
1	small onion, sliced	2 tbsp	light soy sauce
1	green pepper, chopped	1 tsp	chopped fresh ginger
1	sweet red pepper, chopped	¼ cup	apple juice
1 cup	chopped broccoli	1 tbsp	balsamic vinegar
1 cup	fresh or frozen peas	½ tsp	mild curry powder
½ cup	bean sprouts		

In a large wok or skillet, heat both oils together. Add the onion, green and red peppers, broccoli, peas, bean sprouts and snow peas. Stir fry 2 minutes, or until vegetables are tender but not overdone. Stir in cooked spaghetti, soy sauce and ginger; stir-fry another 3 to 4 minutes. In a small bowl, mix together the apple juice, balsamic vinegar and curry powder. Make a hole in the centre of the wok and pour in this mixture, cooking briefly about 3 minutes. Toss everything well to combine.

"See, even with your heels on I'm still taller than you."

Medley of Vegetables

SERVES 6 TO 8

This medley—a tuneful combination of squash, sweet potato, zucchini, broccoli and more—will have you bursting out in song.

3 cups	vegetable stock		1/4 tsp	grated nutmeg
4	cloves garlic, crushed		2	bay leaves
1/2 cup	white wine		1 cup	cubed butternut squash
1/2 cup	chopped fresh parsley		1	small sweet potato, cubed
1/2 cup	chopped fresh basil		1	large potato, cubed
1/4 cup	chopped fresh dill		2	large carrots, cubed
1 tsp	black pepper		1	small zucchini, cubed
1/2 tsp	salt		1 cup	broccoli florets
1/2 tsp	cinnamon		1 cup	cauliflower florets
1/2 tsp	chili powder		1	large red onion, chopped
1/4 tsp	ground cloves		1	red pepper, chopped

Tip
*If you see something labelled **yam** in the grocery store, it is almost certain to be a sweet potato.*

In a large pot, combine stock, garlic, wine, parsley, basil, dill, pepper, salt, cinnamon, chili powder, cloves, nutmeg and bay leaves. Bring to a boil. Reduce to simmer, and add squash, sweet potato, potato and carrots. Cook 5 to 8 minutes, until almost done. Add the zucchini, broccoli, cauliflower, red onion and red pepper. Mix well and cook another 5 to 8 minutes, until all vegetables are tender, but not soft. Remove bay leaves and serve.

Curry Vegetable Stew with White Wine

SERVES 4 TO 6

A great stew to curl up with on a chilly day.
Try it topped with a dollop of plain yogurt.

2 tbsp	olive oil		½ tsp	salt
1	large red onion, quartered		½ tsp	black pepper
2	cloves garlic, minced		1	bay leaf
2	celery stalks, chopped		1	bulb fennel, sliced
3 cups	vegetable stock		4	large carrots, chopped
2 tbsp	mild curry powder		6	medium potatoes, cubed
1 tsp	balsamic vinegar		1	zucchini, chopped
1 tsp	Worcestershire sauce		1	yam, peeled and cubed
1 tsp	dried basil		½ cup	white wine
1 tsp	dried thyme		1 can	(28 oz) stewed tomatoes
½ tsp	cayenne pepper			

In a large pot, heat the oil and sauté the onion, garlic and celery until translucent. Add vegetable stock, curry powder, balsamic vinegar, Worcestershire sauce, basil, thyme, cayenne, salt, pepper and bay leaf. Bring to a boil. Add fennel, carrots, potatoes, zucchini and yam. Reduce heat and simmer about 12 to 15 minutes. Stir in white wine and stewed tomatoes; allow to reduce another 5 minutes. Vegetables should be tender, not overcooked.

Tip
A dash of balsamic vinegar is a great way to liven up a dish that tastes "flat."

Butternut Squash Stew with Maple Syrup and Cinnamon

SERVES 6

Butternut squash is a favourite for many people.
Enjoy its rich texture and sweet flavour in this wonderfully
comforting stew.

2 cups	vegetable stock	1	small yam, peeled and cubed
1 cup	apple juice	2	small carrots, cubed
½ tsp	dried thyme	1	green red pepper, chopped
½ tsp	dried basil	½ cup	broccoli florets
½ tsp	dried rosemary	½ cup	frozen peas
½ tsp	black pepper	½ cup	maple syrup
2 cups	cubed butternut squash	½ tsp	cinnamon
1	medium potato, cubed		

In a large crockpot or soup pot, combine the vegetable stock, apple juice, thyme, basil, rosemary and black pepper. Bring to a boil and reduce to a simmer. Add the squash, potato, yam and carrots. Allow to simmer 15 minutes; then add the red pepper, broccoli and peas. Simmer another 5 minutes and stir in the maple syrup and cinnamon. Mix and allow to simmer another 5 minutes.

Sweet Potato Stew with Fennel and Fresh Mint

SERVES 6

*The orange and green of this dish is a feast for the eyes
as well as the palate.*

2 tbsp	olive oil		1	bay leaf
3	cloves garlic, mined		4	medium sweet potatoes, peeled and chopped
2	celery stalks, chopped		2	large carrots, chopped
1	medium onion, chopped		½	bulb fennel, sliced
2 cups	vegetable stock		2	medium tomatoes, chopped
1 tbsp	balsamic vinegar		1	zucchini, chopped
1 tsp	dried basil		½ cup	white wine
1 tsp	dried oregano		½ cup	chopped fresh mint
½ tsp	dried sage		2 tbsp	honey
½ tsp	dried thyme		½ cup	chopped fresh parsley
½ tsp	sea salt			
½ tsp	black pepper			

In a large pot, heat the oil and sauté garlic, celery and onion until translucent. Add the vegetable stock, balsamic vinegar, basil, oregano, sage, thyme, salt, pepper and bay leaf. Bring to a boil. Add the sweet potato, carrots and fennel. Reduce heat and simmer 12 to 15 minutes. Stir in tomatoes, zucchini, wine, mint and honey; cook, allowing to reduce another 5 minutes. Vegetables should be tender, not overcooked. Add fresh parsley and serve.

Tip

When buying fresh mint, look for unblemished, bright green leaves with a fresh, minty fragrance. Like most herbs, fresh mint is best used right away.

Vegetarian Chili with White Wine and Fresh Herbs

SERVES 4 TO 6

This one's for the vegetarians out there who for years have felt left out of the chili fun on Super Bowl Sunday.

2 tbsp	olive oil	1/2 cup	chopped fresh parsley
2	medium onions, chopped	1/4 cup	chopped fresh basil
2	cloves garlic, minced	2 tbsp	chopped fresh thyme
1 cup	chopped purple cabbage	2 tbsp	chopped fresh oregano
2	celery stalks, chopped	2 tbsp	chili powder
2	carrots, chopped	1 tsp	paprika
1	sweet red pepper, chopped	1/2 tsp	cayenne pepper
1	green pepper, chopped	1	bay leaf
1 can	(28 oz) stewed tomatoes		Salt and pepper to taste
1 cup	apple juice	1	zucchini, chopped
1/2 cup	white wine	1 cup	cooked red kidney beans

Heat olive oil in a large pot. Sauté onions and garlic until translucent. Add cabbage, celery, carrots, red and green peppers; sauté 2 to 3 minutes. Add stewed tomatoes, apple juice, wine, parsley, basil, thyme, oregano, chili powder, paprika, cayenne, bay leaf, salt and pepper. Cook about 5 minutes. Stir in zucchini and kidney beans, and simmer another 10 minutes.

JB of FT on WFD with KK & MJ

The oh-so-fashionable globe-trotting, runway-commentating, FashionTelevision fashionista Jeanne Beker took time out from her busy schedule to reveal the recipe for her famous chili. During the show, I tried to offer my own variations and other assorted suggestions for her chili recipe: she rejected all of them. On camera, she turned to me and said, "No, I wouldn't do that!" I was deflated—but it was all really very funny.

Johanna W. with the Bride of Frankenstein...I think.

Low-Fat Vegetable Stew with White Wine and Fresh Herbs

SERVES 4 TO 6

Try this dish with a fennel, orange and red onion salad.

3 cups	low-fat/low-sodium vegetable stock		1	bay leaf
2	cloves garlic, crushed		1 cup	cubed butternut squash
½ cup	white wine		2	potatoes, cubed
½ cup	chopped fresh basil		2	carrots, chopped
¼ cup	chopped fresh dill		1	zucchini, chopped
1 tsp	black pepper		1 cup	broccoli florets
½ tsp	salt		1 cup	cauliflower florets
½ tsp	ground cinnamon		1	red onion, chopped
½ tsp	ground cloves		1	green pepper, chopped
½ tsp	grated nutmeg		1	red pepper, chopped

In a large pot combine vegetable stock, garlic, wine, basil, dill, pepper, salt, cinnamon, cloves, nutmeg and bay leaf. Bring to a boil. Reduce to medium simmer and add the squash, potatoes and carrots. Cook until dense vegetables are almost tender, about 12 minutes. Add zucchini, broccoli, cauliflower, red onion, and red and green peppers. Mix well and cook another 5 to 8 minutes. Vegetables should be tender, not soft.

Ratatouille with Fennel

SERVES 4 TO 6

*This versatile dish can be served hot or cold,
over pasta or rice, or all on its own.*

2 tbsp	olive oil	1 tbsp	sugar
3	large onions, chopped	½ tsp	dried basil
2	cloves garlic, chopped	½ tsp	dried thyme
1 can	(28 oz) stewed tomatoes	½ tsp	dried oregano
2	large zucchini, chopped	½ tsp	dried rosemary
2	green peppers, chopped	½ tsp	dried mint
1	sweet red pepper, chopped	½ tsp	salt
2 cups	chopped eggplant	½ tsp	black pepper
1 cup	chopped fennel		

In a crockpot or heavy saucepan, heat the oil. Add the onion and garlic and sauté 2 to 3 minutes or until translucent. (Be careful not to burn the garlic.) Mix in the tomatoes, zucchini, green and red peppers, eggplant, fennel, sugar, basil, thyme, oregano, rosemary, mint, salt and pepper. Cook on low heat for approximately 20 minutes, stirring occasionally. Make sure vegetables do not become too mushy.

"Ah, don't feel too bad, Ken, there are always lifts."

Chicken Wok

Grilled Chicken with Apple and Stilton Cheese

SERVES 4

Try cooking this treat on the indoor or outdoor grill

Variation
Replace the chicken with turkey.

4	boneless skinless chicken breast		½ tsp	sea salt
½ cup	apple juice		½ tsp	black pepper
2	apples, cored and quartered		2 heads	romaine lettuce
¼ cup	chopped fresh parsley		1	small red onion, cut into thin slices
2 tbsp	balsamic vinegar		½ cup	shaved carrot
2 tbsp	olive oil		½ cup	crumbled Stilton cheese
2 tbsp	Dijon mustard		8	cherry tomatoes
1 tbsp	wine vinegar			

Grill chicken breasts, basting with 1/4 cup of the apple juice, and turning once, for 15 minutes or until the chicken is cooked through and has grill marks. Remove, allow to cool, and slice. Grill the apple for 5 minutes. In a bowl, make the dressing by combining the remaining 1/4 cup apple juice, parsley, balsamic vinegar, olive oil, Dijon mustard, wine vinegar, salt and pepper. On four plates, place some lettuce, red onion, shaved carrots and Stilton cheese. Put the chicken breasts on top of each salad and divide salad dressing between the four plates. Place 2 cherry tomatoes on the side of each salad.

Grilled Orange Chicken

SERVES 4

Citrus and poultry have always been a dynamite combo.
Lemon accompaniment is always a favourite,
but this orange accent is a nice "twist."

4	skinless chicken breasts, bone-in	1 tbsp	garlic powder
1 cup	orange juice	1 tbsp	onion powder
¼ cup	finely chopped fresh tarragon	1 tsp	black pepper
2 tbsp	grated orange rind	½ tsp	paprika
		2	oranges, sliced

Coat the chicken with the orange juice and place in a dish. In a bowl, combine the tarragon, orange rind, garlic powder, onion powder, black pepper and paprika. Sprinkle three quarters of the mixture evenly over the chicken, cover and refrigerate for at least 3 hours or overnight. Grill chicken on high. After 15 minutes, turn the chicken; add sliced oranges and sprinkle with the remaining herb mixture. Grill chicken and oranges for another 5 minutes. Garnish chicken with grilled oranges.

You Never Know what People Are Going to Say! Number 1

During our very exciting cross-country tour in season five, we got to meet a lot of the public, from St John's and Halifax all the way to Vancouver and Victoria. On one stop, while we were filming the show in Calgary, a woman approached me and said, "You know, you look much better on television."

Sesame Grilled Chicken and Vegetable Kabobs

SERVES 6

Everybody loves kabobs! The sesame gives these a rich,
nutty dimension.

1 1/2 lb	lean chicken breast, cut into 1 1/2-inch cubes	3 tbsp	sesame oil
1	medium zucchini, cut into 1/2 inch rings	1 tsp	garlic powder
		1 tsp	paprika
1	large red onion, cut into thick wedges	1/2 tsp	dried basil
		1/2 tsp	sea salt
1 cup	large cauliflower florets	1/2 tsp	black pepper
1 cup	large broccoli florets	1/2 cup	chopped fresh parsley
1	green pepper, cut into wedges	1 tbsp	sesame seeds
		6	8-inch wooden skewers, soaked in water

Evenly thread the chicken, zucchini, onion, cauliflower, broccoli and green pepper on the skewers. Gently brush on the sesame oil over the skewers. In a bowl, combine garlic powder, paprika, basil, salt and pepper. Sprinkle this mixture over the skewers. Place the skewers on a heated grill for 18 to 20 minutes, turning 4 times to achieve grill marks. When the kabobs have been grilling for 15 minutes, sprinkle with chopped parsley and sesame seeds. Serve immediately.

Grilled Thai Chicken

SERVES 4

Canned coconut milk has almost become a staple in my household. Mixed with curry and chili, the coconut makes this chicken dish an oriental treat. Serve it with curried rice with raisins, followed by chilled oranges with orange sherbet and mint.

3	gloves garlic, minced	1 tsp	black pepper
1	small onion, chopped	1 tsp	Dijon mustard
1 cup	coconut milk	½ tsp	mild curry powder
½ cup	chopped fresh coriander	4	medium boneless
¼ cup	soy sauce		chicken breasts
2 tbsp	chopped fresh ginger	½ cup	chopped green onions

In a blender combine garlic, onion, coconut milk, coriander, soy sauce, ginger, black pepper, Dijon mustard and curry powder. Remove one-fourth of the marinade and set aside for basting. In a shallow baking dish, combine the chicken breasts and the marinade. Sprinkle with green onions and marinate in refrigerator least 15 minutes (longer if possible.) Place chicken on a pre-heated grill and cook, basting with reserved marinade, 10 to 15 minutes or until cooked through.

Tip
Commercial curry powder comes in two styles: "Standard" and "Madras," which is the hotter of the two.

Tip
Curry powder quickly loses its pungency and should be stored in an air-tight container for no longer than 2 months.

Salsa Chicken with Sweet Red Pepper Sauce

SERVES 4

*Colourful and piquant, this dish will have
your taste buds doing the tango!*

2	sweet red peppers, chopped		1 tsp	sugar or sweetener
½ cup	chopped shallots or onion		¼ cup	fresh thyme or 1 tsp dried
¾ cup	mild-to-hot salsa		½ tsp	chili powder
½ cup	chopped fresh parsley or 1 tbsp dried		½ tsp	salt
¼ cup	apple juice		½ tsp	pepper
			4	boneless skinless chicken breasts

In a food processor, or in a bowl with a hand blender, chop the red pepper and shallots. Add salsa, 1/4 cup of the fresh parsley (or 1/2 tsp dried), apple juice and sugar. Blend well. Transfer sauce to a microwave-safe bowl; set aside. In a small mixing bowl, combine thyme, chili powder, salt and pepper. Sprinkle over the chicken. Grill the chicken, turning once, 10 to 15 minutes, depending on the thickness (make sure the chicken has grill marks). Place on a warm serving plate. Microwave the sweet pepper sauce at high, covered, for 2 to 3 minutes. Pour the sauce over the over chicken and sprinkle with the remaining parsley.

A pensive bunny moment.

Herbed Chicken Stuffed with Ham and Mozzarella

SERVES 4

*These chicken roll-ups are terrific teamed with white rice
with olives, garlic, shallots and mushrooms.*

4	boneless chicken breasts		2 tsp	balsamic vinegar
½ cup	chopped fresh parsley			Salt and pepper to taste
¼ cup	finely chopped chives		4 slices	mozzarella cheese
2 tbsp	chopped fresh basil		4 slices	lean cooked ham
1 tbsp	chopped fresh thyme			Toothpicks to secure
1 tbsp	Dijon mustard			Olive oil
2	cloves garlic, chopped			

Pound thin the chicken breasts, and slice in half lengthwise. In a bowl, combine parsley, chives, basil, thyme, Dijon mustard, garlic, balsamic vinegar, salt and pepper. Coat insides of chicken breasts with mixture. Place one slice of mozzarella cheese and one slice of cooked ham inside each chicken breast. Roll the chicken breasts tightly and skewer with toothpicks. Brush with olive oil and grill for 15 minutes, turning occasionally, until completely cooked.

Tip
Prepare the roll-ups the night before, skewer, and store covered in the fridge.

Tip
Sliced ham is considered one of the leaner sandwich meats; however, it is high in sodium.

Roast Chicken with Garlic and Vegetables

SERVES 4 TO 6

Did you know that garlic is classified as a vegetable?
Here it teams up with fellow veggies to impart a wonderful
aroma and flavour to roasted chicken.

2	potatoes, cubed	2 tbsp	chopped fresh rosemary
3 tbsp	olive oil	1 tsp	chopped fresh sage
1	5- to 6-pound roasting chicken, cut in pieces	½ cup	chicken stock
		½ cup	white wine
25	whole cloves garlic, peeled	1 tsp	chili powder
1	medium red onion, cut into large pieces	½ tsp	salt
		½ tsp	pepper
2	medium carrots, chopped		

Start the potatoes by cooking for 5 to 8 minutes in the microwave oven at high setting; set aside. In a wok or skillet, heat oil. Add chicken and sauté for 10 to 12 minutes or until crispy and lightly browned. Transfer chicken pieces to a casserole dish, along with the garlic, onion and carrots. Sprinkle with rosemary and sage. Combine chicken stock and white wine; pour into the casserole dish. Sprinkle with chili powder, salt and pepper. Bake or roast at 400°F for 20 to 25 minutes.

Spicy Chicken Cutlets with Herbs

SERVES 4

Serve this recipe with scalloped potatoes, Caesar salad, and apple pie with vanilla ice cream.

4	boneless skinless chicken breast	½ tsp	dried sweet basil
2	eggs	½ tsp	dried rosemary
¼ cup	flour	½ tsp	dried oregano
½ cup	bread crumbs	½ tsp	dried thyme
1 tsp	garlic powder	½ tsp	pepper
1 tsp	onion powder	½ tsp	cayenne pepper
		2 tbsp	olive oil

Thinly slice chicken breasts or pound until thin. Mix eggs in a bowl and set aside. Spread flour on a wooden surface. In a large baking dish combine the bread crumbs, garlic powder, onion powder, basil, rosemary, oregano, thyme, pepper and cayenne. Coat each chicken breast with flour. Dip floured chicken breasts into eggs until both sides are covered. Next, coat the chicken with bread crumbs. Heat olive oil and gently fry the chicken until flesh is cooked through and outside is golden. Drain on paper towels and serve immediately.

Variation
Try cracker crumbs or unsweetened cereal in place of bread crumbs

Tip
The coating will stick better while cooking if you refrigerate coated chicken, uncovered, for 30 to 60 minutes before cooking

Layered Chicken Shepherd's Pie

SERVES 4 TO 6

This variation on the standard shepherd's pie is quite a treat.
To speed up cooking time, microwave potatoes
at high for 15 minutes and then mash.

6	potatoes, peeled and quartered		1 cup	frozen peas
½ cup	milk		1	green pepper, chopped
½ cup	chopped fresh dill		½ cup	diced celery
3 tbsp	butter		2	cloves garlic, chopped
1 tbsp	vegetable oil		1 tsp	dried sage
1	small onion, chopped		½ tsp	salt
2 cups	chopped chicken		½ tsp	black pepper
1 cup	diced carrots		½ cup	grated mozzarella cheese

In a large pot, boil potatoes in salted water until tender. Drain and let cool slightly. Using a potato masher or ricer, mash potatoes with the milk, dill and butter. Stir with a wooden spoon until potatoes are well combined. In a large skillet, heat the oil. Sauté the onion in oil for 2 to 3 minutes or until translucent. Add the chopped chicken and cook until brown, about 4 minutes. Mix in the carrots, peas, green pepper, celery, garlic, sage, salt and pepper; cook for 2 minutes. In a large, deep non-stick baking dish, make a layer of one-third of the mashed potatoes, then half of the chicken mixture. Repeat, and finish with a layer of mashed potato. Sprinkle with mozzarella cheese. Bake uncovered at 350°F for 10 minutes or until brown on top.

Variation
Replace chicken with lean ground beef.

Low-Fat Option
Instead of butter, mash the potatoes with some of the potato cooking water or low-fat sour cream.

Low-Fat Option
Before adding vegetables, remove chicken and drain off the oil, then return to skillet.

Kenny's Favourite Chicken and Spinach Roll-Up

Serves 4

*My roll-ups are among the most popular and most requested recipes on **What's for Dinner?** As always, feel free to experiment with ingredients— you can substitute lower-fat turkey breast for the chicken.*

Tip
Try chopping garlic with a little salt; the minced garlic won't stick to the knife. Just remember to alter the salt in the recipe.

	Juice of 1 lemon
1 cup	chopped spinach
2	cloves garlic, chopped
½ cup	chopped fresh parsley
½ cup	sour cream
¼ cup	Dijon mustard
1 tsp	pepper
½ tsp	salt
½ tsp	dried basil

½ tsp	dried thyme
4	large boneless skinless chicken breasts
	Toothpicks for securing
6	slices Swiss cheese
4	thin slices cooked turkey breast
4	slices lemon

In a bowl, combine 1 tsp of the lemon juice, the spinach, garlic, parsley, sour cream, Dijon mustard, half the pepper, the salt, basil and thyme. Gently pound the chicken breasts flat between sheets of plastic wrap. Spread the sauce on the chicken. Top each breast with a slice of Swiss cheese and a slice of turkey. Cut remaining 2 slices of cheese in half and set aside. Roll up the chicken breasts and secure with toothpicks. Arrange in a non-stick baking dish and top each roll-up with a half slice of Swiss cheese and a slice of lemon. Bake uncovered at 375°F for 20 to 25 minutes, or until chicken is no longer pink inside. Sprinkle with remaining pepper and lemon juice and serve immediately.

Variation
Replace Swiss cheese
with emmenthal or
mozzarella.

Tip
When buying
asparagus, choose
thin stalks over thick,
which become tough
and stringy when
cooked.

Tip
Buy lemons at peak
season when they're
cheapest, squeeze the juice
and freeze it in ice-cube
trays; transfer to plastic
bags when frozen
and store up to
6 months.

Chicken and Asparagus Roll-ups with Dijon and Basil

SERVES 4 TO 6

*This roll-up is a pleasing variation on my favourite
(see previous page). Serve it with a mixed green salad
or grilled vegetables.*

2	cloves garlic, minced		½ tsp	black pepper
½ cup	chopped fresh parsley		4	boneless skinless chicken breasts, pounded thin
½ cup	chopped fresh basil			
¼ cup	Dijon mustard		6	slices Swiss cheese
¼ cup	sour cream		8	asparagus spears
½ tsp	salt			Toothpicks for securing

In a bowl, mix garlic, parsley, basil, mustard, sour cream, salt and pepper. Spread the sauce on the chicken breasts. Top each breast with a slice of Swiss cheese and 2 asparagus spears. Roll up the chicken breasts and secure with toothpicks. Cut the remaining 2 cheese slices in half. Arrange chicken in a non-stick baking dish and top each roll-up with a half slice of Swiss cheese. Bake at 350°F for 25 minutes or until chicken is cooked. To get 6 portions, slice roll-ups prior to serving.

Curried Chicken and Vegetables with Raisins and Cloves

SERVES 4

I love cloves as much as I love curry! By the way, the clove—the fragrant, unopened flower bud of the tropical evergreen clove tree—is considered one of the world's most important spices.

2 tbsp	vegetable oil	1	sweet potato, cubed
4	chicken breasts	1	zucchini, diced
1	red onion, chopped	¾	cup raisins
2	large carrots, diced	2 tbsp	curry powder
2	medium potatoes, peeled and diced	2 tbsp	soy sauce
2	cloves garlic	½ tsp	pepper
1 ½ cups	chopped fresh coriander	½ tsp	cinnamon
1 ½ cups	chopped fresh parsley	1	bay leaf
1 ½ cups	chicken stock	1	medium onion, whole
		3	cloves

Heat oil in a wok or large skillet and gently sauté chicken until golden. Remove chicken and sauté red onion 2 to 3 minutes. Add carrots and potatoes, and sauté 8 to 10 minutes until slightly cooked. In a bowl, combine coriander, parsley, chicken stock, sweet potato, zucchini, raisins, curry powder, soy sauce, pepper and cinnamon; add to the skillet. Place bay leaf on the whole onion and pierce with cloves. Place in middle of mixture in skillet, add chicken, and simmer approximately 15 to 20 minutes. Remove onion. Serve immediately in a large bowl or platter.

Variation
Replace chicken with chick-peas and chicken stock with vegetable stock for a vegetarian version.

Tip
Coriander and cilantro are one and the same. It is also referred to as Chinese parsley, and was one of the first herbs to be grown in America.

Poached Chicken in White Wine with Fresh Herbs

SERVES 4

Poaching is so easy, and so healthy, that I recommend it for preparing any type of meat or seafood. Most people poach in water, but using wine and stock makes for absolute perfection.

2 cups	chicken stock		2 tbsp	chopped fresh thyme
1 cup	white wine		2 tbsp	balsamic vinegar
2	onions, finely chopped		½ tsp	salt
1	red pepper, chopped		½ tsp	pepper
¼ cup	chopped fresh basil		1	bay leaf
2	cloves garlic, crushed		4	boneless skinless
2 tbsp	chopped fresh rosemary			chicken breasts

In a large deep skillet, bring to a boil the stock, wine, onions, red pepper, basil, garlic, rosemary, thyme, balsamic vinegar, salt, pepper and bay leaf. Reduce heat and simmer for about 10 minutes. Add the chicken and poach 12 to 15 minutes or until meat is no longer pink inside.

You Never Know what People Are Going to Say! Number 2

Once, in downtown Toronto, I was approached by a gentleman who said, "Excuse me, are you Ken Kostick?" I smiled back and said, "Yes." He then said, "I have to say, you are the worst waste of airtime on television." A wee bit flustered, but without skipping a beat, I responded with, "Thank you very much for your comments," and walked on. Perhaps surprised by my response, he apologized and we proceeded to have a very pleasant chat.

Coq Au Vin

SERVES 4 TO 6

This chicken in wine recipe is an old standard made easier.

2 cups	chicken stock		3 lbs	stewing chicken pieces
2 cups	red wine		½ lb	bacon, chopped
1 tsp	dried dill		1	onion, chopped
½ tsp	dried basil		2	cloves garlic, minced
½ tsp	dried oregano		½ cup	chopped carrots
½ tsp	dried thyme		½ cup	chopped celery
1	bay leaf		1 tbsp	butter
½ tsp	salt		1 cup	sliced mushrooms
½ tsp	black pepper			

In a crock pot or a large saucepan, bring to a boil the stock, wine, dill, basil, oregano, thyme, bay leaf, salt and pepper. Reduce to a simmer. Microwave chicken at high for approximately 5 to 7 minutes. Meanwhile, in a large non-stick skillet, sauté bacon until soft. Add the onion, garlic, carrots and celery; sauté about 10 minutes until partially cooked. Remove vegetables and set aside. Melt butter in skillet and sauté chicken for 10 minutes. Add to the sauce with reserved vegetables; simmer another 10 to 15 minutes or until liquid is reduced and chicken is cooked. Add mushrooms and cook another 8 to 10 minutes. Discard bay leaf and serve.

Chicken Stew Italian-Style with Herbs

SERVES 4 TO 6

*What makes this stew Italian? Well, it's the lovely thick
accent of garlic, tomato and oregano!*

2 tbsp	olive oil
4 lbs	chicken legs and breasts
1	red onion, chopped
2	cloves garlic, chopped
1 cup	chopped mushrooms
2	tomatoes cut into chunks
1 can	(28 oz) stewed tomatoes
1 cup	chicken stock
¾	cup red wine

1 tbsp	chopped fresh rosemary
1 tsp	tomato paste
½ tsp	dried basil
½ tsp	dried thyme
½ tsp	dried oregano
½ tsp	dried sage
1	bay leaf
½ tsp	salt
½ tsp	black pepper

In a wok or skillet, heat 1 tbsp of the olive oil and sauté chicken until brown, about 4 minutes each side. Remove chicken and set aside. To the skillet add the remaining 1 tbsp oil; sauté the onion and garlic for 2 to 3 minutes or until translucent. Add the mushrooms and sauté another minute. Mix in the tomatoes, stock, wine, rosemary, tomato paste, basil, thyme, oregano, sage, bay leaf, salt and pepper. Add the chicken and simmer another 20 to 25 minutes, or until chicken is no longer pink inside. Discard the bay leaf. When serving, spoon the sauce on top.

Caught in the act!

Chicken Stew Spanish-Style

SERVES 4 TO 6

*For a saucy variation, add salsa and serve while
samba-ing to serenading señoritas.*

3 tbsp	olive oil		1	green pepper, chopped
3	chicken breasts		1 can	(28 oz) stewed tomatoes
3	chicken legs		1 cup	mild or hot salsa
½ tsp	salt		1 cup	red wine
½ tsp	pepper		1 cup	red kidney beans
2 tbsp	chili powder		½ cup	frozen corn
1	red onion, chopped		½ cup	brown sugar
4	cloves of garlic, minced		½ tsp	cayenne pepper
1	red pepper, chopped		1	bay leaf

Heat 1 tbsp of the oil in a skillet. Place chicken on wax paper; shake salt and pepper on it. Place chicken in skillet and cook until it begins to brown, turning once. Sprinkle chili powder on top of chicken and put a lid on the skillet. Continue to cook the chicken until it turns a very rich red. In a separate deep pot that can be placed in the oven, heat the remaining 2 tbsp oil and sauté onion, garlic, red and green peppers for 2 to 3 minutes. Add tomatoes, salsa, wine, kidney beans, frozen corn, brown sugar, cayenne and bay leaf. Bring to a boil and reduce immediately to a simmer. Add chicken to pot and cook in the oven at 350°F for 15 to 20 minutes.

Variation
Replace chicken with chick-peas and navy beans.

Tip
Refrigerate leftover beans and use within five days in salads, stir-fries and soups.

Turkey in Applesauce and Cinnamon

SERVES 2 TO 4

*Try serving this scrumptious dish with
garlic mashed yams and coleslaw.*

2 tbsp	olive oil	½ cup	apple juice
2	boneless skinless turkey breasts	½ cup	chopped fresh mint
½ tsp	salt	1 tbsp	balsamic vinegar
½ tsp	pepper	1 tsp	Worcestershire sauce
2	apples, cored and chopped	1	bay leaf
1 cup	applesauce	½ tsp	ground cinnamon
		¼ tsp	ground cloves

In a wok or large skillet, heat the olive oil. Sprinkle the turkey breasts with salt and pepper; sauté turkey about 10 minutes, turning once. In a shallow baking dish, mix apples, applesauce, apple juice, mint, balsamic vinegar, Worcestershire sauce, bay leaf, cinnamon and cloves. Place turkey in dish and bake at 350°F, occasionally basting with the sauce, for 10 to 15 minutes or until turkey is cooked through.

Turkey Stir-Fry with Grapefruit

SERVES 2 TO 4

Be adventurous! This unusual combination of flavours has been consistently popular since I first served this to hungry guests some years ago. It's best served over fragrant rice, garnished with mint and parsley.

2 tbsp	olive oil	1 cup	bean sprouts
2 cups	sliced or chopped turkey	½ cup	grapefruit juice
1	red onion, sliced	½ cup	chopped fresh parsley
1	sweet red pepper, sliced in strips	¼ cup	chopped fresh mint
		½ tsp	black pepper
1	sweet green pepper, sliced in strips	¼ tsp	salt
2	medium carrots, sliced	1	grapefruit, peeled and cut into bite-sized pieces
1	cup chopped broccoli	2	tbsp grapefruit zest for garnish
½ tsp	chopped fresh ginger		

In a wok or large skillet, heat the oil over high heat. Stir-fry the chopped turkey in the hot oil until slightly golden at the edges. Remove the turkey and set aside. In the same skillet, stir-fry the onion, red and green peppers, carrots, broccoli and ginger for 5 minutes. Add the bean sprouts and stir-fry 1 to 2 minutes. Reduce heat to medium and stir in the turkey, grapefruit juice, parsley, mint, pepper and salt, and cook about 2 minutes. Add the grapefruit and cook, stirring, for 1 minute. Arrange on plates and garnish with grapefruit zest.

Variation
Replace turkey with sliced chicken breast.

Low-Fat Option
Cook vegetables in grapefruit juice instead of oil.

Tip
The high heat of the wok and the oil seals in juices and preserves colour and flavour.

Turkey Swiss-Cheese Roll-Ups in Tomato Sauce

SERVES 4

*More and more **What's for Dinner?** viewers are switching from chicken to lower-in-fat turkey (I know because I get their letters!). Enjoy this favourite with a spinach salad and soup.*

Variations
Replace the parsley with coriander. Add 1/4 cup red wine with the tomatoes.

1	large turkey breast, sliced into 4 cutlets	1 can	(28 oz) stewed tomatoes
2 tbsp	Dijon mustard	2	cloves garlic, minced
4	slices ham	½ cup	chopped fresh basil or
4	slices Swiss cheese		½ tsp dried
1 cup	chopped fresh parsley	1 tsp	black pepper
2 tbsp	olive oil	½ tsp	salt

Lay the turkey cutlets out and spread each one with 1/2 tbsp of the Dijon mustard. Top each with one piece of ham and one slice of Swiss cheese. Sprinkle the parsley evenly over the turkey breasts. Roll up tightly and secure with toothpicks. Heat the olive oil in a large sauté pan or frying pan, and brown the turkey roll-ups on all sides, about 4 minutes altogether. Add the tomatoes, garlic, basil, pepper and salt. Allow to simmer for 15 minutes, or until turkey is done and sauce is reduced. Serve roll-ups and tomato sauce with rice or pasta.

Grilled Cornish Hen with Sesame and Coriander

SERVES 4

Delight guests at your next dinner party with Cornish hens. This recipe can be done on your indoor grill; it will fill your home with the wonderful aroma of grilled fowl.

½ cup	vegetable soup stock		½ tsp	black pepper
½ cup	chopped fresh coriander		2	large (about 2 lbs each) Cornish game hens, cut in half
2 tbsp	sesame oil			
2 tbsp	balsamic vinegar			
½ tsp	onion powder		2 tsp	sesame seeds
½ tsp	garlic powder		½ cup	fresh parsley
½ tsp	chili powder			

In a large mixing bowl combine the stock, 1/4 cup of the coriander, sesame oil, balsamic vinegar, onion powder, garlic powder, chili powder and pepper. Brush the Cornish hens evenly with about half the mixture and set aside in the refrigerator for at least 2 hours. Set grill at high, and place the hens skin-down get grill marks; grill for 15 minutes, turning about every 5 minutes, occasionally basting with the remaining sauce. Sprinkle with sesame seeds and the remaining 1/4 cup of coriander. Continue to grill another 10 minutes or until no pink is showing under the wings. Remove and place on a platter with parsley arranged around outer edges. If any sauce is left, brush on at the end.

> **Tip**
> *Because of the high oil content, sesame seeds turn rancid quickly and are best stored in an airtight container in a cool dark place.*

The Best of Beef!

Ayyyy! Oyyyy!

Mama Kostick's Barbecue Hamburgers

SERVES 4 TO 6

*This is my favourite, basic hamburger recipe: it's so good
that you never need to try another. However,
if you want to impress yourself, try adding other herbs,
spices, blue cheese—whatever you want!*

2 lbs	ground beef	1 tbsp	Dijon mustard
1	onion, chopped fine	1 tsp	dried basil
1	clove garlic, minced	½ tsp	chili powder
1	egg, beaten	½ tsp	salt
2 tbsp	ketchup	½ tsp	pepper

In a large bowl, mix together ground beef, onion, garlic, egg, ketchup, Dijon mustard, basil, chili powder, salt and pepper. Use your hands to shape mixture into 4 or 6 patties. Grill or fry patties for 10 to 12 minutes, or until well done. Place on hamburger buns and use your favourite toppings.

Mama Kostick

Helen Kostick became quite a popular fixture on *What's for Dinner?* Whenever my mother made guest appearances, viewers got a kick out of her deadpan gaze, her cheeky comments about *my* recipes, and the fact that she always gave Mary Jo a run for her money. On one episode, she really got out of hand—when she was first introduced, the first thing out of her mouth was, "Ken, dear, you left your face-lift cream in the dressing room." It's hard to get respect from dear old Mom.

Chili Meatloaf with Sour Cream and Coriander

SERVES 6

*This chili meatloaf might be reminiscent of what your mother
made for you decades ago: this one, however,
is much more flavourful.*

Low-Fat Option
*Replace the ground
beef with the much
lower-in-fat ground
turkey.*

2 lbs	ground beef	½ cup	chopped fresh coriander
1	egg, beaten	½ cup	sour cream
1	small onion, chopped	1 tbsp	chili powder
1	sweet red pepper, chopped	½ tsp	dried thyme
½ cup	dry bread crumbs	½ tsp	salt
½ cup	chopped fresh parsley	½ tsp	black pepper

In a large bowl, combine ground beef, egg, onion, red pepper, bread crumbs, parsley, coriander, sour cream, chili powder, thyme, salt and pepper. Mix well and turn into a 9 inch x 4 inch baking dish. Bake at 350°F for 25 to 30 minutes, or until meatloaf is done in the centre and browned on top.

Not bad, considering....

The Easiest Beef Stew

SERVES 4 TO 6

*This dish, which appeared way back in the very first episode of **What's for Dinner?**, is easily one of the most requested recipes.*

3 tbsp	olive oil	½	sweet red pepper, chopped
1	medium onion, chopped	½	small zucchini, chopped
1 ½ lbs	stewing beef, cubed	1	bay leaf
3	medium potatoes, cubed	1 tsp	dried basil
2 cups	chicken or beef stock	½ tsp	dried rosemary
1 cup	dry red wine	½ tsp	salt
2	carrots, coarsely chopped	½ tsp	pepper
4	celery stalks, chopped		

In a large pot, heat oil. Sauté onion for 2 to 3 minutes or until translucent. Add meat and cook 5 to 7 minutes more. Meanwhile, place potatoes in a microwave-safe dish and microwave for 1 to 2 minutes at high. To the pot, add potatoes, stock, wine, carrots, celery, red pepper, zucchini, bay leaf, basil, rosemary, salt and pepper. Simmer for 15 to 20 minutes or until vegetables are tender and liquid is reduced.

Ah, Mary Jo, do you have to strangle me every time we take a photo?

Beef Stew with Red Wine and Fresh Herbs

SERVES 4 TO 6

*This is a scrumptious **ragout**; serve it with green beans,
mashed potatoes and large hunks of Italian or French bread.*

2 tbsp	olive oil	1 cup	beef stock or
1 lb	lean stewing beef		vegetable stock
1	medium onion, chopped	½ cup	red wine
2	cloves garlic, chopped	½ cup	chopped black olives
2	large potatoes, cubed	½ cup	chopped fresh basil
2	carrots, cubed	2 tbsp	chopped fresh oregano
1	small zucchini, cubed	2 tbsp	chopped fresh rosemary
1	sweet red pepper, chopped	2 tbsp	Dijon mustard
2	celery stalks, chopped	1 tbsp	Worcestershire sauce
1 can	(28 oz) stewed tomatoes	1	bay leaf
1 cup	chopped sun-dried	½ tsp	hot sauce
	tomatoes		Salt and pepper to taste

In a large, deep skillet, heat 1 tablespoon of the oil; sauté beef 3 to 5 minutes or until browned. Remove from heat and set aside. In the same skillet, heat the remaining 1 tbsp oil. Add onion and garlic, and sauté for 2 to 3 minutes or until onion is translucent. Add potatoes, carrots, zucchini, red pepper and celery; sautéing for 8 to 10 minutes or until vegetables are tender, but not overdone. Add tomatoes, stock, wine, olives, basil, oregano, rosemary, Dijon mustard, Worcestershire sauce, bay leaf, hot sauce, salt and pepper. Bring to a boil, add the beef, and reduce to simmer. Simmer for 15 to 20 minutes or until liquid has reduced.

Variations
For a vegetarian version of this stew, omit the beef. Replace the beef with firm white fish, such as cod.

Tip
If you don't have wine, replace it with balsamic vinegar or more stock.

Stir-Fried Orange Beef with Fennel and Tarragon

SERVES 2 TO 4

*Beef with orange, fennel and tarragon is a most pleasing dish,
especially when served with heapings of spinach and
mushroom salad and a light, lemony soup.*

Variation
For a more Asian dish,
replace fennel with
bok choy and bean
sprouts.

2 tbsp	olive oil		½	yellow pepper, sliced
1 lb	sirloin, thinly sliced		½ cup	chopped green onions
1 cup	broccoli florets		¼ cup	chopped fresh tarragon
1 cup	cauliflower florets		½ tsp	salt
2	carrots, cut lengthwise and halved		½ tsp	pepper
½ cup	chopped fennel		¼ cup	orange juice
½	red pepper, sliced		1 tbsp	grated orange zest

In a wok or deep sauté pan, heat 1 tbsp of the oil. Add sirloin and cook 5 to 6 minutes, or until brown. Remove from pan and set aside. In the pan, heat the remaining 1 tbsp oil. Add broccoli, cauliflower, carrots, and fennel; sauté for 3 to 4 minutes or until tender. Add red and yellow peppers, green onions, tarragon, salt and pepper; sauté for another 4 minutes or until peppers are tender. Add beef, orange juice and zest, and stir-fry another 2 minutes. Be careful not to overcook the vegetables. Serve over rice or noodles.

Tip
*Meat stocks, such
as beef and chicken,
are recommended for
long-cooking recipes, as
vegetable and fish stocks
lose flavour if simmered
longer than
30 minutes.*

Mediterranean Beef with Tomatoes in Red Wine

SERVES 4 TO 6

Whenever any of my recipes calls for canned stewed tomatoes,
and you'd prefer to use fresh tomatoes, substitute
2 plum tomatoes, 1 teaspoon tomato paste and
2 cups water or vegetable stock.

2 tbsp	vegetable oil	½ cup	chopped fresh basil
1 ½ lbs	cubed stewing beef	½ cup	red wine
1	red onion, chopped	2 tbsp	chopped fresh rosemary
2	cloves garlic, chopped	½ tsp	salt
2	carrots, sliced and halved	½ tsp	pepper
1 can	(28 oz) stewed tomatoes	1	bay leaf

In a deep sauté pan, heat 1 tbsp of the oil. Brown beef in the hot oil 3 to 5 minutes; remove and set aside. In the pan, heat the remaining 1 tbsp oil. Add onion and garlic, and sauté for 1 to 2 minutes or until translucent. Add carrots and cook another 2 minutes. Add tomatoes, basil, wine, rosemary, salt, pepper and bay leaf, and bring to a boil. Reduce heat, add beef and cover. Simmer for 10 to 15 minutes or until liquid is reduced and beef is done.

Beef and Mushroom Brochettes Marinated in White Wine

SERVES 4

Brochette is a fancy word for shish kabob! You'll need 2 hours prep time to marinate the meat.

	MARINADE		BROCHETTES
½ cup	white wine	1 lb	round steak, cubed
2	cloves garlic, crushed	4	wooden skewers, soaked in water
1 tbsp	dried basil		
1 tbsp	dried thyme	2 cups	large whole button mushrooms
1 tbsp	dried oregano		
1 tbsp	balsamic vinegar	1	red onion, cut into wedges
1 tbsp	Worcestershire sauce		
½ tsp	salt		
½ tsp	pepper		

To make marinade

In a shallow baking dish, combine wine, garlic, basil, thyme, oregano, vinegar, Worcestershire sauce, salt and pepper. Mix well. Place the beef in the marinade and let sit for a minimum of 2 hours.

To prepare brochettes

Preheat the grill to medium-high. Thread beef on skewers, alternating with mushrooms and onion. Once all 4 skewers are ready, grill on barbecue, turning 4 times, for 10 to 12 minutes or until beef is done and vegetables have grill marks.

Thai Beef Brochette with Coconut Milk and Honey

SERVES 4

*This extremely tasty Thai treat is best served on a bed of
fragrant or basmati rice, accompanied by chicken lemongrass
soup and a dish of green mango salad. However, it will do
just fine with any rice, and any green salad.*

4	wooden skewers	½ tsp	cayenne pepper
1 cup	unsweetened coconut milk	½ tsp	black pepper
½ cup	chopped fresh coriander	1 ½ lbs	top round, cut into
¼ cup	soy sauce		½-inch slices
¼ cup	liquid honey	8	cherry tomatoes
2	cloves garlic, minced	2	large red onions, cut into
1 tsp	freshly chopped ginger		quarters

Soak wooden skewers in water for 30 minutes. Make marinade in a food processor by combining coconut milk, coriander, soy sauce, honey, garlic, ginger, cayenne
and black pepper. Purée until marinade is creamy. Set aside 1/2 cup marinade for
basting. Transfer remaining marinade to a shallow baking dish. Thread the beef on
the skewers, alternating with tomatoes and onion: 2 tomatoes and 2 pieces of
onion per skewer. Marinate skewers at least 20 minutes, covered and refrigerated,
turning occasionally. Set grill to medium high. Grill skewers, basting with reserved
marinade, for 5 to 7 minutes or until beef is done and grill marks appear.

Mandarin Orange Beef with Tarragon

SERVES 2

*The small mandarin orange adds a piquant taste to these
New York steaks, but feel free to substitute Florida oranges,
if you so desire.*

Variation
*Replace New York steak
with a cheaper cut, such
as a flank steak, marinate
at least four hours to
ensure tenderness.*

½ cup	mandarin orange juice		2 tbsp	grated orange zest
¼ cup	liquid honey		½ tsp	salt
¼ cup	soy sauce		½ tsp	pepper
2 tbsp	Worcestershire sauce		2	New York steaks
2 tbsp	chopped fresh tarragon or 1 tsp dried		4	mandarin oranges, sliced

In a food processor, blend the orange juice, honey, soy sauce, Worcestershire sauce, tarragon, 1 tbsp of the orange zest, salt and pepper. Purée until marinade is creamy. Set aside 1/4 cup marinade for basting. Transfer remaining marinade to a shallow baking dish. Trim fat from steaks; punch holes on both sides with a fork. Marinate steaks in baking dish for 60 minutes, covered and refrigerated, turning occasionally. Once steaks are ready, set grill to medium high. Grill steaks, basting with reserved marinade, for 4 to 6 minutes on each side, depending on your taste. Remove from grill and place on a platter. One minute before serving, lightly grill orange slices. Garnish steaks with orange slices and more fresh tarragon, and serve immediately.

Round Steak Marinated in Honey and Beer

SERVES 6

Cooking with spirits is one of my favourite summertime activities. Go wild and try a light Belgian beer in the marinade for a superb steak. And be certain to leave yourself at least 4 hours before cooking time to marinate the steaks.

1 cup	beer	4	cloves garlic, chopped fine
½ cup	soy sauce	2	round steaks, ½-inch
¼ cup	liquid honey		thick

In a blender or food processor, combine the beer, soy sauce, honey and garlic. Pulse until marinade is well blended. Set aside 1/2 cup marinade for basting. Transfer remaining marinade to a large, shallow baking dish. Trim fat from steaks; punch holes on both sides with a fork. Marinate steaks in baking dish for 4 hours, covered and refrigerated, turning periodically. Once steaks are ready, set grill to medium high. Grill steaks for 6 to 8 minutes on each side, occasionally basting with reserved marinade. Once done, remove from grill and serve immediately

Spicy Salisbury Cutlets with Sweet Onion Relish

SERVES 2 TO 4

I love this entrée—serve it with garlic-dill mashed potatoes
and an endive blue-cheese salad, and you're set.

Variations

If you prefer, use red wine instead of apple juice. Replace the ground beef with ground pork, or ground chicken or turkey.

1 1/2 lbs	lean ground beef		1/2 tsp	garlic powder
1/2	sweet red pepper, finely chopped		1/2 tsp	paprika
			1/2 tsp	black pepper
1/2	green pepper, finely chopped		1/2 tsp	dried basil
			1/4 tsp	dried thyme
1/2 cup	dry bread crumbs		1	egg, lightly beaten
1/4 cup	Dijon mustard		2 tbsp	vegetable oil
1/2 tsp	chili powder		3	red onions, chopped
1/2 tsp	hot pepper flakes		1/2 cup	apple juice
1/2 tsp	onion powder		2 tbsp	liquid honey

In a large mixing bowl, combine the ground beef, red and green peppers, bread crumbs, Dijon mustard, chili powder, hot pepper flakes, onion powder, garlic powder, paprika, black pepper, basil, thyme and egg; mix well. Shape the mixture into 4 patties. In a skillet, heat 1 tbsp of the oil; sauté Salisbury steaks, without burning, about 5 minutes on each side, until golden brown. Remove from pan and keep warm in oven. In the skillet, heat the remaining 1 tbsp oil; sauté the red onions for 3 minutes. Add the apple juice and honey; sauté until onions are golden brown. Serve onion relish over the Salisbury steaks.

T-Bone Steak with Papaya Relish

SERVES 2

Papaya makes this beef dish a truly tropical delight.

2	T-bone steaks	½ cup	warm water
2	papayas, mashed	2 tbsp	honey
2 tsp	olive oil	½ tsp	salt
1 ½ cup	orange juice	½ tsp	black pepper
½ cup	chopped fresh coriander		

Tip
As well as adding tropical flavour, the papaya contains enzymes that tenderize the meat.

Pierce both sides of each steak with a fork. Cover the top of each steak with 1/3 of the mashed papaya and set aside. In a saucepan, heat the oil on medium heat. Add the remaining papaya, orange juice, 1/4 cup of the coriander, water, honey, salt and pepper. Stir until mixture thickens. Keep relish warm. Broil steaks, 5 to 6 minutes for rare, 7 to 8 minutes for medium. One minute before steaks are done, place a spoonful of the relish on each steak. Place steaks on a serving plate with remainder of the relish and garnish with remaining 1/4 cup coriander.

Okay, I've had it...now I'm downright ornery.

Variation
Replace the steak
with boneless
chicken breasts.

Low-Fat Option
Replace butter with
vegetable stock,
and honey with
apple juice.

Tip
Always salt meat
towards the end of
cooking, or salt will
drain some of the
juices.

Grilled Beef Tenderloin with Mushrooms in Red Wine Sauce

SERVES 2

*This is one of those dishes to savour with a good bottle
of red wine—if you are drinking wine with the meal,
be sure to use the same wine for cooking.*

MARINADE		SAUCE	
½ cup	soy sauce	2 tbsp	butter
¼ cup	honey	1	small red onion, chopped
2	cloves garlic, crushed	1 cup	sliced button mushrooms
2 tbsp	Dijon mustard	½ cup	chopped sweet red pepper
1 tbsp	Worcestershire sauce	½ cup	red wine
1 tbsp	balsamic vinegar	½ tsp	salt
½ tsp	chopped fresh ginger	½ tsp	black pepper
2	beef tenderloin steaks		

To make marinade
In a mixing bowl, combine soy sauce, honey, garlic, Dijon mustard, Worcestershire sauce, balsamic vinegar and ginger. Reserve 1/4 cup for basting and set aside. Transfer rest of marinade to a shallow baking dish and marinate steaks for 30 minutes, covered and refrigerated, turning occasionally.

To make sauce
In a skillet, melt butter. Sauté onion, mushrooms and red pepper until onion is translucent and vegetables are soft. Stir in the red wine and allow to simmer. Add salt and pepper. Keep sauce warm.

Once steaks are marinated, set grill to medium high. Grill steaks, basting occasionally with reserved marinade: 5 to 6 minutes for rare, 7 to 8 minutes for medium. Remove from heat and place on platter. Pour sauce over steak, garnish with chopped fresh parsley, and serve immediately.

Beef Steaks Sautéed in Tomato and White Wine Sauce

SERVES 4

*Reminiscent of the famous Steak Diane, this beef dish
with tomato, wine and herbs is even more flavourful
and every bit as fancy.*

3 tbsp	olive oil	½ cup	chopped fresh parsley
1 ½ lbs	round steak	½ tsp	dried thyme
1	medium onion, minced	½ tsp	dried rosemary
2	cloves garlic, chopped	½ tsp	cayenne pepper
1 can	(28 oz) crushed tomatoes	½ tsp	salt
1 cup	white wine	½ tsp	pepper

In a large skillet, heat 2 tbsp of the oil and sauté the steak 2 to 3 minutes on each side. Remove from pan and set aside. Add remaining 1 tbsp oil to the pan and sauté the onion and garlic for 2 to 3 minutes, or until onion is translucent. Stir in the tomatoes, wine, parsley, thyme, rosemary, cayenne, salt and pepper. Stir constantly and scrape any brown bits from the bottom of the pan for added flavour. Reduce heat and simmer the sauce for 10 minutes, stirring occasionally, until it is reduced by one-fourth. Return the steaks to the pan and cook for about 5 minutes, depending on the degree of doneness desired. Turn the meat frequently to allow it to absorb the flavours of the sauce.

Tangy New York Steaks with Red Pepper and Apple Sauce

*Fire up the grill! (Or the broiler.) Here's another version of my favourite New York steak recipe from the third season of **What's for Dinner?***

4	5-oz New York steaks, or	½ tsp	pepper
	2 10-oz New York steaks	1	red pepper, chopped
	cut to make 4 portions	1	small red onion,
1 tbsp	chopped fresh rosemary		chopped finely
½ tsp	garlic powder	1	apple, sliced
½ tsp	dried thyme	1 cup	apple juice
½ tsp	dried basil	2 tbsp	honey
½ tsp	red pepper flakes	1 tsp	olive oil
½ tsp	salt		

Trim the New York steaks of any excess fat. In a mixing bowl, combine the rosemary, garlic powder, thyme, basil, red pepper flakes, salt and pepper. Spread herb mixture on wax paper. Coat both sides of steaks; let sit, covered and refrigerated, for at least 2 hours. Meanwhile, in a food processor, combine red pepper, onion, apple, apple juice, honey and oil; purée until smooth. Transfer to a saucepan. Set heat to high and allow to boil. Reduce heat and simmer for about 10 minutes or until liquid has reduced by half. Keep sauce warm. When steaks have marinated, set grill to medium high. (You can also use the broiler in your oven.) Grill or broil to desired doneness: 5 to 6 minutes for rare, 7 to 8 minutes for medium. Remove from grill and place on a platter. Pour sauce on top and serve immediately.

Calf's Liver and Onions with White Wine Sauce

SERVES 2

*Liver and onions is a comfort-food staple. This version
introduces a bit of urban chic to a classic.*

1 lb	calf's liver	2	cloves garlic, minced
½ tsp	salt	½ cup	white wine
½ tsp	pepper	1 tbsp	liquid honey
2 tbsp	butter	½ tsp	dried basil
2 tbsp	olive oil	½ cup	chopped fresh coriander
2	large red onions, sliced		

On wax paper, salt and pepper each side of the liver. Slice liver and set aside. In a
large skillet, melt butter and heat 1 tbsp of the oil; sauté onions for 2 to 3 minutes
or until translucent. In a separate skillet or sauté pan, heat remaining 1 tbsp oil;
cook liver and garlic for 5 to 7 minutes. Add 1/4 cup of the wine. Simmer another
5 to 7 minutes. Meanwhile, in the skillet with onions, add the remaining 1/4 cup
of wine, honey and basil; cook for another 2 minutes, stirring constantly. When
liver is done, transfer to platter and cover with onion wine sauce. Garnish with
coriander and serve.

Feeding Time!

The camera crew resembled a school of sharks at certain times of the
day: once the show was taped, they'd attack, downing all the food. In
year one, one camera guy gained 20 pounds in one month. It was heart-
ening to know he loved the food, even if it was liver and onions at 8:30 in
the morning!

Spinach Wrapped in Veal and Lemon

SERVES 4 TO 6

Either wrapped or rolled, these spinach-stuffed veal delights are great as appetizers or as a main course.

Variation
For a vegetarian version, replace veal with six 1/4-inch thick eggplant slices.

Low-Fat Option
Sauté in vegetable stock rather than olive oil.

2 tbsp	olive oil	1/4 cup	lemon juice
2 cups	chopped spinach		Salt and pepper to taste
2	cloves garlic, chopped	6	thin veal cutlets
1 tbsp	chopped fresh basil	1/2 cup	dry white wine
1/2	sweet red pepper, chopped	1	lemon, cut into 6 slices

In a saucepan, using 1 tbsp of the olive oil, sauté the spinach, garlic, basil, red pepper, half the lemon juice, salt and pepper. Cook, stirring occasionally, about 5 minutes or until spinach wilts. Remove from heat and allow to cool before dividing the mixture into six portions. Wrap one portion in each piece of veal. Secure with toothpicks. Heat remaining 1 tbsp olive oil in sauté pan and sauté the veal, turning occasionally, about 3 minutes or until meat starts to turn white. Add the remaining lemon juice and white wine. Place lemon slices on top of veal. Simmer another 4 minutes or until the wine has reduced by half and the meat is cooked.

Veal Poached in Raspberry and White Wine

SERVES 4

*Poached veal is light and delicious. Serve this with the
Watercress and Blue Cheese Salad on page 8.*

1 cup	white wine	½ tsp	dried thyme
½ cup	raspberry juice	½ tsp	salt
1	small red onion, finely chopped	½ tsp	pepper
1	clove garlic, finely chopped	4	large veal cutlets
½ tsp	dried basil	1 cup	frozen raspberries
		½ cup	chopped fresh parsley

In a large sauté pan, combine the wine, juice, onion, garlic, basil, thyme, salt and pepper. Bring to a boil and reduce to simmer. Poach the veal in this liquid about 10 minutes. Add the raspberries and parsley. Cook another 5 minutes or until the veal is completely done.

Variation
Replace veal with chicken breast and poach at least 10 minutes longer.

In between seasons, at my cabin, with my life-long friend Joe. (He lives close by in a cabin he built 45 years ago.)

Other Great Meat Dishes

In the dressing room at Rainbow Stage, during the run of Crazy for You 1999.

Garlic and Honey Pork Brochettes

SERVES 6

My pork brochettes take only 10 minutes to prepare; however, allow 30 minutes to soak the skewers in water, and 15 to 30 minutes to marinate the brochettes before grilling.

6	wooden skewers	1 tsp	chopped fresh ginger
½ cup	orange juice	½ tsp	black pepper
½ cup	chopped fresh coriander	1 ½ lbs	lean pork, cut into
¼ cup	soy sauce		½-inch slices
¼ cup	honey	10 to 12	cherry tomatoes
¼ cup	chopped fresh parsley		

Soak wooden skewers in water for 30 minutes. In a food processor, purée orange juice, coriander, soy sauce, honey, parsley, ginger and black pepper. Pour marinade into a shallow baking dish. Thread the pork and cherry tomatoes onto skewers, using 2 tomatoes per skewer. Marinate brochettes in baking dish, covered and refrigerated, at least 15 minutes (the longer, the better). Grill brochettes, turning occasionally, 12 to 15 minutes, until they are cooked thoroughly and have grill marks.

The Hazards of a Cooking Show!

We did a barbecue episode during year three, when we introduced the little patio off the kitchen. Someone (I won't name names) had turned on the grill's side plate without telling me. I put down my mitt and *it caught fire!* Heroically, I put out the fire and saved the set—and Mary Jo.

Lemon Grilled Pork Chops with Mint

SERVES 4

*This is a delicious and healthy meal: pork is a good source
of thiamin with generous amounts of B vitamins,
and is a good source of infection-fighting zinc. Lemon is
practically calorie-free and is thought to help boost
immunity to diseases and heal wounds!*

1 cup	soy sauce		2 tbsp	grated lemon rind
½ cup	lemon juice		2 tbsp	honey
1	clove garlic, finely chopped		2 tbsp	vegetable oil
			½ tsp	ground black pepper
¼ cup	chopped fresh mint		4	pork chops
¼ cup	chopped fresh parsley			
¼ cup	chopped chives or green onion			

Variation
*Replace pork with
lamb chops or
boneless chicken
thighs.*

In a large baking dish, mix the soy sauce, lemon juice, garlic, mint, parsley, chives
or green onion, lemon rind, honey, vegetable oil and pepper. Reserve 1/4 cup of
marinade and set aside. Place pork chops in marinade; cover with plastic wrap and
marinate refrigerated a minimum of 2 hours (this can be done the night before).
When the pork chops have been marinated, grill on barbecue set at high, turning
once and basting occasionally with reserved marinade, for about 15 minutes or
until cooked through.

Pork Chops with Pineapple and Fresh Herbs

SERVES 4

*This scrumptious dish first appeared in season three,
on our Flintstones episode—if I remember correctly,
I was Fred and Mary Jo was a great, big Dino.*

Low-Fat Option
*Replace the pork
chops with 4 skinless
boneless chicken or
turkey breasts.*

2 tbsp	olive oil	½ cup	chopped fresh parsley
4	large pork chops	½ cup	white wine
1	large red onion, chopped	¼ cup	chopped fresh coriander
2	cloves garlic, minced	2 tbsp	chopped fresh thyme
2	carrots, halved and sliced	2 tbsp	chopped fresh oregano
1 can	(28 oz) stewed tomatoes	1	bay leaf
1 cup	fresh chopped pineapple or 1 can pineapple	½ tsp	salt
		½ tsp	black pepper

In a deep sauté pan or skillet, heat the oil; brown the pork chops on both sides, 8 to 10 minutes or until nearly cooked through. Remove from pan and set aside. Sauté the onion and garlic in the pan, stirring, until onion is translucent, being careful not to burn them. Add carrots and sauté another 2 minutes. Stir in tomatoes, pineapple, parsley, wine, coriander, thyme, oregano, bay leaf, salt and pepper. Place the pork chops in the sauce, cover and simmer 10 minutes or until meat has turned white. Discard bay leaf and serve.

Potato Ham Casserole with Sour Cream and Spinach

SERVES 4 TO 6

When you add spinach to anything, it instantly becomes Florentine-style!

Low-Fat Options
Replace Cheddar and mozzarella cheeses with the low-fat variety. Replace ham with cooked turkey.

2 cups	shredded spinach	1 tsp	paprika
2 cups	chopped cooked ham	½ tsp	salt
1 cup	shredded Cheddar cheese	½ tsp	pepper
4	large eggs, beaten	4	large potatoes, thinly sliced
1	medium onion, chopped	½ cup	shredded mozzarella cheese
½ cup	sour cream		
½ cup	cream		
½ cup	diced sweet red pepper		

In a large mixing bowl, combine spinach, ham, Cheddar cheese, eggs, onion, sour cream, cream, red pepper, paprika, salt and pepper. Mix well. Line the bottom and sides of a non-stick baking dish with sliced potatoes. Sprinkle with 1/4 cup of the mozzarella cheese. Add another layer of potatoes. Add ham mixture and bake at 375°F for 25 to 30 minutes. Sprinkle the top with remaining 1/4 cup mozzarella and bake for another 5 minutes or until cheese is melted and golden.

Pork Stew with Red Wine and Olives

SERVES 4 TO 6

Always use black olives for this dish, not unripened green olives; green olives impart a much different flavour.

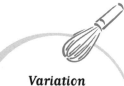

Variation
Replace the pork with stewing beef.

Low-Fat Option
Replace the pork with chopped turkey.

½ lb	bacon, chopped		¼ cup	chopped fresh basil
1	large red onion, chopped		1 tbsp	chopped fresh rosemary
2	cloves garlic, minced		½ tsp	salt
3 lbs	boneless pork, cut into 1-inch pieces		½ tsp	black pepper
			1	bay leaf
1 can	(19 oz) stewed tomatoes		1 cup	pitted and chopped black olives
2 cups	vegetable stock			
1 cup	red wine			

In a frying pan, sauté bacon, onion, garlic and cubed pork for 8 to 10 minutes or until pork is cooked through. Add tomatoes, stock, wine, basil, rosemary, salt, pepper and bay leaf; bring to a boil. Reduce heat and simmer about 15 or 20 minutes. Stir in olives and simmer another 5 minutes.

Spicy Pork Stew with Vegetables and White Wine

SERVES 4 TO 6

Serve this delicious, zesty stew with bruschetta and corn soup.

2 tbsp	olive oil	1	red pepper, diced
2 lbs	stewing pork, in 1-inch cubes	1	green pepper, diced
		1	zucchini, chopped
1	small onion, chopped	½ cup	white wine
2	garlic cloves, chopped	¼ cup	chopped fresh basil
2	carrots, chopped	2 tbsp	chopped oregano
2	celery stalks, chopped	1 tsp	chopped jalapeño pepper
1 can	(28 oz) stewed tomatoes	½ tsp	salt
2	medium potatoes, cubed	½ tsp	black pepper
2 cups	vegetable stock		

In a large pan, heat olive oil; brown pork evenly for about 4 to 6 minutes each side. Remove pork and set aside. In the pan, sauté the onion, garlic, carrots and celery until onion is translucent. Return pork to pan, and stir in tomatoes, potatoes, stock, red and green peppers, zucchini, wine, basil, oregano, jalapeño, salt and pepper. Heat to a boil; reduce heat and simmer for 20 to 25 minutes or until all the flavours have cooked through.

Tip
Always wear cloves when peeling, seeding or chopping jalapeño peppers: they can sting.

Irish Lamb Stew with Beer

SERVES 4 TO 6

*This hearty stew with beer and fresh herbs was our salute
to St. Patrick's Day during our third season. For a delicious
accompaniment, serve with potato pancakes and green beer.
(By the way, you don't have to use Guinness beer;
I just wanted to keep the recipe as Irish as the name Padric.)*

2 tbsp	olive oil	1 cup	vegetable stock
2 lbs	lean stewing lamb, cubed	1 cup	Guinness beer
1	medium onion, chopped	½ cup	chopped fresh basil
2	cloves garlic, minced	1 tbsp	chopped fresh oregano
2	potatoes, cubed	1 tbsp	chopped fresh thyme
2	carrots, cubed	1 tbsp	Worcestershire sauce
2	celery stalks, chopped		Salt and pepper to taste
1	zucchini, diced	2	bay leaves
1	green pepper, chopped	½ tsp	cayenne pepper
1 can	(28 oz) stewed tomatoes		

In a large soup pot over medium heat, heat 1 tbsp of the oil; brown the lamb in batches for about 5 minutes each batch. Remove lamb and set aside. In the same pot, heat the remaining 1 tbsp oil. Add the onion, garlic, potatoes, carrots, celery, zucchini and green pepper; sauté until vegetables are tender but not overdone. Add tomatoes, stock, 1/2 cup of the beer, basil, oregano, thyme, Worcestershire sauce, salt, pepper, bay leaves and cayenne pepper. Bring to a boil; reduce heat to simmer. Stir in lamb and remaining 1/2 cup beer. Cover and cook another 10 to 20 minutes. Before serving, remove and discard bay leaves.

Curry Lamb and Vegetable Stew

SERVES 4 TO 6

For a richer, more robust flavour, add 1/2 cup dry red wine to this Caribbean special.

2 tbsp	olive oil	1	zucchini, cubed
2 lbs	lamb, cubed	½ cup	chopped fresh parsley
1	large red onion, chopped	¼ cup	chopped fresh basil
2	large carrots, cubed	2 tbsp	soy sauce
2	medium potatoes, cubed	2 tbsp	mild curry powder
2 cups	chicken stock	½ tsp	black pepper
2	cloves garlic, minced	½ tsp	cinnamon
1	sweet potato, cubed	1	bay leaf

Variation
Replace the lamb with cubed chicken or turkey.

In a large skillet, heat the oil; brown the lamb on all sides. With a slotted spoon, transfer the lamb to a bowl. In the oil, sauté the onion, carrots and potatoes for about 5 minutes. Stir in the stock, garlic, sweet potato, zucchini, parsley, basil, soy sauce, curry powder, pepper, cinnamon and bay leaf. Add lamb to the skillet; simmer covered, stirring occasionally, for 15 to 20 minutes or until all ingredients are tender. Discard the bay leaf and serve.

Lamb Poached in Vegetable Tomato Sauce

SERVES 4 TO 6

Poached lamb is easy, healthy and delicious,
especially with the wonderful herbs and vegetables
called for in this recipe. Enjoy!

2 tbsp	olive oil		½ tsp	dried sage
3 lbs	stewing lamb, cubed		½ tsp	salt
6	plum tomatoes,		1 tsp	black pepper
1 tbsp	tomato paste		2	bay leaves
1 ½ cups	water		1	zucchini, diced
½ cup	red wine		½ cup	chopped green onion
½ cup	freshly chopped parsley		½ cup	shaved carrot
¼ cup	chopped fresh basil		½ cup	chopped fennel
½ tsp	dried thyme			

In a large pan, heat the oil. Add the lamb and brown for about 5 minutes. Add the tomatoes, tomato paste, water, red wine, parsley, basil, thyme, sage, salt, pepper and bay leaves. Bring to a boil; reduce heat to medium and add zucchini, green onion, carrot and fennel. Simmer for 15 to 20 minutes or until lamb is cooked and vegetables are tender.

Baked Lamb Chops with Fresh Rosemary

SERVES 4

*Rosemary and lamb were made for each other! (By the way,
if you'd rather, use black olives instead of green ones.)*

4	large lamb chops	½ cup	green olives, pitted
2 tbsp	olive oil	½ cup	peas
2	cloves garlic, minced	½ cup	red wine
1	large onion, chopped	2 tbsp	fresh rosemary, chopped
2	large carrots, chopped	1 tsp	dried oregano
2	tomatoes, chopped	1 tsp	dried thyme
1	sweet red pepper	1 tsp	black pepper
1 cup	vegetable stock	½ tsp	salt
1 cup	spinach, chopped		

Preheat oven to 400°F. In a large pan, gently sauté lamb chops in oil for 3 to 4 minutes on each side, or until browned. Transfer lamb to baking dish; add the garlic, onion, carrots, tomatoes, red pepper, stock, spinach, olives, peas, wine, rosemary, oregano, thyme, black pepper and salt. Bake for 20 to 25 minutes or until vegetables are done.

The lovely Johanna (our talented food stylist).

Lamb Chops and Cranberries with Red Wine

SERVES 4

*This recipe requires a grill or broiler; be sure to reserve
some sprigs of fresh rosemary for garnish.*

MARINADE

3/4 cup	unsweetened cranberry juice
1/2 cup	red wine
1	small onion, finely chopped
2	cloves garlic, crushed
2 tbsp	chopped fresh rosemary or 2 tbsp chopped fresh basil
1 tbsp	red wine vinegar
1 tbsp	lemon juice
1/2 tsp	black pepper
1/4 tsp	salt
8	thick lamb chops

GARNISH

1/2 cup	chopped fresh parsley
1/4 cup	fresh cranberries (if in season) or frozen
1/4 cup	chopped olives

To make the marinade

In a large pan, mix together cranberry juice, wine, onion, garlic, rosemary or basil, vinegar, lemon juice, pepper and salt; mix well. Reserve 1/4 cup of marinade for basting.

Place lamb chops in pan and marinate for at least 20 minutes. Basting with reserved marinade, broil lamb for 5 to 8 minutes per side, depending on degree of done-ness desired. Garnish lamb with rosemary sprigs, parsley, fresh cranberries and olives.

Seared Spring Lamb with Fresh Mint and White Wine

SERVES 4

Serve this fresh take on lamb and mint sauce with rice or roasted potatoes.

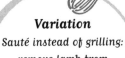

Variation
Sauté instead of grilling: remove lamb from marinade and gently sauté in 1 tbsp olive oil for 2 to 3 minutes per side.

½ cup	white wine	1 tsp	dried basil
¼ cup	chopped fresh mint	3	bay leaves
¼ cup	vegetable stock	1	large sweet red pepper, chopped
3	cloves garlic, minced		
2	shallots, finely chopped	4	large lamb chops or
2 tbsp	lemon juice		6 small, thick lamb chops

In a shallow baking dish, mix together wine, mint, stock, garlic, shallots, lemon juice, basil and bay leaves. Remove 4 tbsp of the mixture; purée the remaining mixture with the red pepper in a food processor or blender. Reserve 1/2 cup of the red pepper sauce to use later as garnish. To make marinade, combine puréed mixture with the 4 tbsp of wine-herb mixture; marinate lamb chops for 10 minutes. Grill lamb for 2 to 3 minutes per side. Garnish with reserved red pepper sauce.

New Zealand Spring Lamb with Fennel and Red Pepper Sauce

SERVES 2 TO 4

*Spring lamb means it is usually 3 to 5 months old
(any lamb over a year old is called mutton, which has a much
stronger flavour and is less tender). The method here provides
two ways to prepare this dish: grilling or sautéing. If grilling,
prepare the sauce and marinade in advance.*

2	small onions, finely chopped	2 tbsp	lemon juice
2	cloves garlic, minced	1	bay leaf
½ cup	white wine	1	sweet red pepper, chopped
¼ cup	chopped fresh parsley	4	large lamb chops
		½	fennel bulb, sliced

To grill

In a shallow baking dish, mix together the onions, garlic, wine, parsley, lemon juice and bay leaf. Remove 3 tbsp of the mixture and purée the remaining mixture with the red pepper in a food processor. Reserve 1/2 cup of the puréed mixture for garnish. To make marinade, stir remaining purée into the herb-wine mixture. Marinate lamb in a baking dish 10 to 15 minutes. Grill lamb 2 to 3 minutes per side; grill fennel slices until it has grill marks. Arrange lamb and fennel on plates and garnish with reserved red pepper purée.

To sauté

In a large skillet, gently sauté the lamb chops in 2 tbsp of olive oil for 2 to 3 minutes each side. Add the onions, garlic, wine, parsley, fennel, lemon juice, bay leaf and red pepper. Reduce heat and simmer 5 to 8 minutes. Discard bay leaf and serve.

Tip
Defrost lamb in the refrigerator overnight or longer to retain all its juices and flavour.

From the Deep Blue Sea

Easy Fish Stew

*This is so easy, it should become part of your
cooking repertoire!*

4 cups	vegetable stock		1/2 tsp	dried thyme
1 can	(28 oz) stewed tomatoes		1/2 tsp	dried sage
2	celery stalks, chopped		1/2 tsp	chili powder
2	carrots, chopped		1/2 tsp	black pepper
2	cloves garlic, chopped		1	bay leaf
1	small red onion, cut into rings		1	small swordfish steak, cut into 1-inch cubes
1	red pepper, sliced		1	small tuna steak, cut into 1-inch cubes
1	small zucchini, cubed			
1 cup	tomato juice		1 can	(10 oz) clams, drained and rinsed
1/4 cup	red wine (optional)			
1/2 tsp	dried oregano		1/4 cup	chopped fresh parsley

In a large soup pot, combine the stock, tomatoes, celery, carrots, garlic, onion, red pepper, zucchini, tomato juice, wine, oregano, thyme, sage, chili powder, black pepper and bay leaf. Simmer over medium heat 20 minutes or until the liquid has reduced by half. Add the swordfish, tuna and clams, and simmer another 5 to 6 minutes. Be careful not to overcook the seafood. Remove bay leaf. Serve hot, sprinkled with fresh parsley.

Crab Cakes with Fresh Herbs

SERVES 4

Make sure you use fresh seafood for this recipe—crab cakes this good deserve the real thing!

CRAB CAKES		DIP	
1 lb	fresh crabmeat	1 cup	yogurt
2	celery stalks, finely chopped	1/2 cup	chopped fresh parsley
2	eggs	2 tbsp	chopped chives
1/2 cup	chopped red pepper	1 tbsp	balsamic vinegar
1/4 cup	bread crumbs	1/2 tsp	salt
1/4 cup	chopped fresh parsley	1/2 tsp	black pepper
2 tbsp	chopped fresh dill		
2 tbsp	chopped fresh basil		
2 tbsp	chopped fresh oregano		
1 tbsp	Dijon mustard		
1/2 tsp	paprika		
1/2 tsp	salt		
1/2 tsp	black pepper		

To make crab cakes

In a large mixing bowl, combine crabmeat, celery, eggs, red pepper, bread crumbs, parsley, dill, basil, oregano, Dijon mustard, paprika, salt and pepper. Mix well and shape into 4 large crab cakes. Place them in a baking dish and broil for 4 to 5 minutes on each side.

To make dip

In a small mixing bowl, combine the yogurt, parsley, chives, balsamic vinegar, salt and pepper. Mix well and serve over crab cakes.

Shrimps with Tomatoes and Zucchini

SERVES 4

*A great dish to whip up when summer garden tomatoes
and squash are in their prime.*

2 tbsp	olive oil		2	large tomatoes, chopped
1	small red onion, chopped		½ cup	vegetable stock
1 cup	cubed zucchini		½ cup	chopped fresh parsley
1	small green pepper, chopped		½ tsp	sea salt
16	large shrimp, peeled and deveined		½ tsp	black pepper

In a large deep sauté pan, heat the oil; gently sauté the onion, zucchini and green pepper about 4 minutes or until tender. Add the shrimp, tomatoes and stock. Cook for 5 minutes turning the shrimp occasionally. Add the parsley, salt and pepper, and cook for another 2 minutes or until shrimps have turned pink.

St Andrews by the Sea in a Housecoat

St. Andrews by the Sea, in New Brunswick, was one of the loveliest spots on our Canada tour, despite the fact that Emperor Ken had no clothes! You see, the airline misplaced my luggage so, for two days, I dined out and shot *What's for Dinner?* in a lovely white terry housecoat, courtesy of the hotel.

Variation
For a vegetarian dish, replace the shrimps with button mushrooms.

BEST OF WHAT'S FOR DINNER?

Shrimp Stir-Fry with Ginger and Peppers

SERVES 4

Ginger is an amazing root—packing a huge flavour punch,
a little goes a long way. Here it jazzes up veggies and
shrimp in a great, quick meal.

2 tbsp	olive oil	2	large carrots, sliced diagonally
½ cup	chopped green onion	½ tsp	dried basil
2	cloves garlic, minced	½ tsp	black pepper
1 tbsp	chopped fresh ginger	¼ cup	soy sauce or tamari sauce
12 to 16	large jumbo shrimp, shelled and de-veined	2 tbsp	honey
2	sweet red peppers, sliced	2 tbsp	crushed almonds
1	green pepper, sliced	1 tsp	sesame seeds
2	celery stalks, sliced on diagonal		

In a wok or deep skillet, heat the oil; sauté the onion and garlic about 2 minutes. Add the ginger and cook 2 minutes. Add the shrimp and sauté for 2 to 3 minutes. Remove shrimp from wok and set aside. Combine the red and green peppers, celery, carrots, basil and pepper in the wok; make a well in the centre and add the soy sauce and honey. Stir-fry for about a minute. Add in the seafood; toss well. Garnish with sesame seeds and almonds.

Low-Fat Option
Sauté in 1/4 cup
vegetable stock
instead of olive oil.

Tip
Always peel ginger, but be
careful to remove only the
skin—the delicate flesh
under the surface is the
most flavourful.

Shrimp with Lemon and Orange Sauce

SERVES 4

The sauce for these shrimps is a teasingly sweet delight.

1 tbsp	olive oil
1	small onion, chopped
12	large jumbo shrimp, peeled and deveined
2	tbsp grated orange and lemon zest combined
½ tsp	pepper

¼ cup	orange juice concentrate
2 tbsp	lemon juice
½ cup	sour cream
2 tbsp	liquid honey
½ tsp	dried mint
¼ tsp	salt

In a skillet, heat the olive oil, and sauté onion for 2 minutes. Add the shrimp, 1 tbsp of the orange and lemon zest, and pepper; sauté for 1 to 2 minutes. Stir in orange juice concentrate and lemon juice and simmer half a minute. Add sour cream, honey, mint, remaining 1 tbsp zest and salt, and simmer for 5 minutes until the liquid reduces and thickens.

At the Geminis: dressed to accept! (We lost.)

BEST OF WHAT'S FOR DINNER?

Calamari in Spicy Tomato Sauce

SERVES 4 TO 6

*Trendy calamari is also quite delicious. Don't be afraid
to prepare it at home! This recipe makes it easy.*

3 tbsp	olive oil		1/4 cup	chopped fresh coriander
2	cloves garlic, minced		1/4 cup	freshly squeezed lemon juice
1	small red onion, minced		2 tsp	liquid honey
4 cups	calamari rings		1/2 tsp	red pepper flakes
1 can	(28 oz) stewed tomatoes, diced		1/2 tsp	tomato paste
1/2 cup	dry red wine			Lemon wedges, for garnish
1/2 cup	tomato juice			

In a large sauté pan or skillet, heat the oil and sauté the garlic and onion until onion is translucent, about 2 minutes. Add the calamari and sauté 3 to 4 minutes, or until it turns white. Stir in the tomatoes, wine, tomato juice, coriander, lemon juice, honey, red pepper flakes and tomato paste. Reduce heat to medium and simmer 8 to 10 minutes, until calamari is tender. Garnish with lemon wedges. Serve with French bread for dipping.

Shrimps and Scallops in Lemon Butter Sauce

SERVES 4

*Once the shrimps and scallops in sauce are done, serve
on a bed of fettuccine (or any pasta), or mix the pasta
directly in the sauté pan.*

16 oz	fettuccine	1/4 cup	chopped fresh parsley
1/4 cup	butter	1/4 cup	white wine
1	small onion, chopped	4 tbsp	lemon juice
12	jumbo shrimp, peeled and deveined	1 tbsp	Worcestershire sauce
12	jumbo scallops	1 tbsp	chopped fresh chives
1/4 cup	vegetable stock	1	lemon, sliced
		1 tsp	grated lemon rind

In a large pot, cook fettuccine in boiling salted water until tender. Meanwhile, in a deep skillet, melt the butter until foaming. Sauté onion for 2 to 3 minutes or until translucent. Add the shrimp and scallops, and sauté 4 to 5 minutes. Add vegetable stock, parsley, wine, lemon juice, Worcestershire sauce, chives and lemon; simmer another 5 minutes or until wine has reduced. Serve over pasta and garnish with lemon rind.

Mussels in White Wine with Vegetables and Fresh Herbs

SERVES 4

Serve this mussel entrée with plenty of French bread,
so your guests can sop up the delicious broth.

1 tbsp	olive oil	1 can	(19 oz) stewed tomatoes
1	onion, sliced	1/2 cup	white wine
2	cloves garlic, coarsely chopped	1/2 cup	chopped fresh parsley
2	large carrots, cut into strips	1/4 cup	chopped fresh basil
4	celery stalks, cut on the diagonal	1/4 cup	chopped fresh dill
1 cup	chopped zucchini	1 tsp	pepper
1 cup	chopped mushrooms	1/2 tsp	salt
1/2 cup	chopped fennel	1/2 tsp	chopped hot peppers
		4	dozen mussels, cleaned and debearded

In a deep skillet or crockpot, heat the oil and sauté the onion, garlic, carrots, celery, zucchini, mushrooms and fennel for 2 to 3 minutes. Add the tomatoes, white wine, parsley, basil, dill, pepper, salt and hot peppers. Bring to a boil and reduce heat. Simmer about 10 to 15 minutes. Add the mussels and cover. Cook 2 to 3 minutes, or until the shells have opened (discard any mussels that do not open). Serve in shallow soup bowls, ladling the wine sauce over the mussels.

Grilled Scallops with Asparagus and Grapefruit

SERVES 4

Try these tangy scallops with a side dish of bananas
grilled with brown sugar and lime

½ cup	soy sauce
½ cup	chopped fresh parsley
¼ cup	grapefruit juice
2 tbsp	finely chopped garlic chives
2 tbsp	grated grapefruit rind
1 tbsp	honey
1 tsp	rice wine vinegar
1 tsp	chopped ginger
1 tsp	chopped hot green chili peppers

1 tsp	white pepper
	Juice of 1 lemon
14	large or jumbo scallops
12	asparagus spears, ends trimmed
1	grapefruit, sliced
1	lemon, cut into wedges
4	bamboo skewers, soaked in water

The court jester during an uncharacteristic moment of angst.

In a large mixing bowl, combine soy sauce, parsley, grapefruit juice, chives, grapefruit rind, honey, rice wine vinegar, ginger, hot peppers, white pepper and lemon juice. Marinate scallops, covered and refrigerated, in this mixture for 1 hour. Skewer scallops, alternating with asparagus, folded grapefruit slices and lemon. Grill for 5 minutes or until scallops turn white and have sear marks.

Baked Orange Roughy with Herbs and Spices

SERVES 4

If you've never tried roughy—a relatively inexpensive
but tasty white fish—now's the time.

1/4 cup	flour		1/2 tsp	curry powder
2	eggs		1/2 tsp	dried sage
1/2 cup	bread crumbs		1/2 tsp	chili powder
1 tsp	garlic powder		1/2 tsp	salt
1 tsp	onion powder		1/2 tsp	black pepper
1 tsp	paprika		1/4 tsp	cayenne pepper
1/2 tsp	dried rosemary		4	large orange roughy fillets
1/2 tsp	cinnamon		1	lemon, quartered for
1/2 tsp	dried parsley			garnish

In a small bowl, mix eggs and set aside. Spread the flour on a wooden surface. In a large baking dish, combine bread crumbs, garlic powder, onion powder, paprika, rosemary, cinnamon, parsley, curry powder, sage, chili powder, salt, pepper and cayenne pepper. Coat the fish in flour. Dip floured fillets into the egg mixture until both sides are covered. Next, coat the fish in seasoned breadcrumbs. Bake in pre-heated 350°F oven for 20 minutes or until golden. Garnish with lemon wedges.

Tip
When buying fillets,
the general rule is
4 to 5 ounces per
serving.

Oven-Baked Herbed Sea Bass

SERVES 4

Serve this dish with a mixed green salad
and garlic mashed potatoes.

2	eggs		1 tsp	salt
1 tsp	dried sweet basil		1 tsp	black pepper
1 tsp	dried thyme		4	sea bass fillets
1 tsp	dried oregano		½ cup	bread crumbs
1 tsp	onion powder		1 tbsp	parsley
1 tsp	garlic powder		1 tbsp	olive oil
1 tsp	paprika		1 tsp	lemon juice
½ tsp	cayenne pepper			

In a large mixing bowl, beat the eggs; set aside. In a small bowl, combine basil, thyme, oregano, onion powder, garlic powder, paprika, cayenne pepper, salt and pepper. Dip the sea bass in the eggs until both sides are fully coated. Reserve about one-fourth of the dried herb mixture; sprinkle the rest evenly over fish to coat. Combine reserved dry herb mixture with bread crumbs, parsley, olive oil and lemon juice; press fish in breadcrumb mixture, coating both sides well. Bake in a preheated 350°F oven for 15 minutes or until browned, turning once.

Tip

Paprika is a powder made from ground sweet red peppers. Hungarian paprika is considered the best and is similar to cayenne.

Poached Raspberry Sole with White Wine

SERVES 2 TO 4

Want to impress a special someone?
Serve up this romantic dish with its shades of passionate red.
Results guaranteed.

1 tbsp	oil		1/4 cup	chopped fresh basil
1	small onion, chopped		1 tsp	black pepper
	or 2 shallots, chopped		1/2 tsp	salt
1 cup	cranberry juice		1	bay leaf
1/4 cup	white wine		2	large sole fillets
1/4 cup	chopped fresh mint		2 cups	fresh or frozen raspberries

In a skillet, heat the oil. Sauté onion until translucent. Mix in cranberry juice, white wine, mint, basil, pepper, salt and bay leaf. Bring to boil and then reduce heat to simmer. Poach sole in liquid, covered, for 8 minutes or until sole is white. Add raspberries and cook another 5 minutes. Serve fish fillets whole or sliced, with poaching mixture.

> **Tip**
> Remember, fish continues to cook after it's removed from the pan, so be careful not to overcook.

Sole Poached in Red Wine with Mushroom and Gorgonzola Sauce

SERVES 4

This is arguably the best sole dish prepared on **What's for Dinner?**—*the sauce of gorgonzola cheese and Dijon mustard is an irresistible combination with the subtle sole poached in wine.*

Tip

Saffron is best bought whole because the powder can easily be altered without detection; however, it is expensive and should be used sparingly.

Tip

When you buy fillets, look for firm texture, moist appearance and a fresh odour.

POACHING LIQUID

2 cups	vegetable or fish stock
1 cup	red wine
1/2 cup	chopped fresh dill
1/4 cup	chopped fresh Italian parsley
2	cloves garlic, chopped
	Juice of one lemon
1 tsp	lemon rind
1 tsp	black pepper
1/2 tsp	salt
1/4 tsp	saffron
1	bay leaf
4	sole fillets

SAUCE

2 tbsp	butter
1	small shallot, chopped
2 cups	chopped button mushrooms
1/4 cup	red wine
1/2 cup	gorgonzola cheese
1/4 cup	cream
2 tbsp	Dijon mustard
1/2 tsp	dried basil
1/2 tsp	salt
1/2 tsp	pepper

To poach fish

In a deep sauté pan, heat stock and wine to a boil. Mix in dill, parsley, garlic, lemon juice, lemon rind, pepper, salt, saffron and bay leaf. Add sole and poach at a simmer 5 to 7 minutes (10 to 15 minutes if the fish is frozen) depending on thickness.

To make sauce

In a saucepan or small sauté pan, melt butter. Cook shallot until translucent. Add mushrooms and cook about 5 minutes. Stir in red wine and allow to reduce, about 2 minutes. Add the gorgonzola, cream, Dijon mustard, basil, salt and pepper. Cook on low, stirring until thickened. Serve over fish.

"You've got to be kidding, right?"

Grilled Tuna with Tangy Orange Sauce

SERVES 4

*Although this recipe calls for the tuna to be marinated for
15 minutes, marinate for longer if time allows—as much as
2 hours—covered and refrigerated.*

Tip
*Don't salt the fish
before cooking. Salt
draws the moisture
out of fish and
toughens it.*

1 1/4 cups	orange juice with pulp	2 tbsp	grated orange rind
1 cup	pieces of peeled orange (about 2 oranges)	1/2 tsp	black pepper
2	tuna steaks cut in half	1/4 tsp	salt
1 tbsp	olive oil	1/2 cup	sour cream
2	green onions, chopped	1/2 cup	table cream or half-and-half cream
1/2 cup	white wine		Grilled orange slices for garnish
2 tbsp	chopped fresh dill		

In a shallow glass dish, combine 1 cup of the orange juice and 1/2 cup of the orange pieces. Marinate the tuna in orange mixture for approximately 15 minutes, turning occasionally. In a medium saucepan over medium heat, heat oil and sauté onions until tender. Add wine and raise heat, cooking for 3 to 4 minutes to reduce liquid. Add remaining 1/4 cup of orange juice, remaining 1/2 cup of orange pieces, dill, orange rind, pepper and salt, and simmer 10 minutes. Stir in sour cream and cream; allow liquid to thicken, stirring constantly. Do not boil or sour cream will curdle. Keep sauce warm. Grill tuna, occasionally brushing with marinade, 3 to 4 minutes on each side until tuna turns light. Serve tuna with sauce, garnished with orange slices.

Poached Salmon Steaks in Orange and Tarragon

SERVES 4

*My poached salmon in orange and tarragon is delicious
served with rice and steamed spinach.*

1 tbsp	olive oil	¼ cup	freshly chopped tarragon
2	shallots, chopped	1 tbsp	chopped orange rind
2	cloves garlic, chopped	1 tsp	black pepper
½ cup	white wine	½ tsp	salt
1 cup	orange juice	1	bay leaf
1 cup	vegetable stock	4	medium salmon steaks
½ cup	chopped fennel	½ cup	chopped fresh parsley

In a large skillet, heat the oil; sauté shallots and garlic until transparent. Add wine and allow to reduce by half. Add orange juice, stock, fennel, tarragon, orange rind, pepper, salt and bay leaf. Bring liquid to a boil; reduce heat to a simmer and add salmon steaks. Cover and poach until fish turns pink, 6 to 8 minutes. Garnish with parsley.

Variation
*Other thick cuts of
fish like swordfish,
salmon or monkfish
can also be used.*

Salmon and Swordfish Kabobs with Red Peppers and Onion

SERVES 4

This recipe calls for 8 skewers; if you're using wooden ones,
please be sure to soak them in water for at least
15 minutes before threading with fish and vegetables
and placing on the grill.

½ cup	lemon juice
½ cup	chopped fresh dill
3	cloves garlic, chopped or puréed
1 tsp	sugar
1 tsp	paprika
½ tsp	salt
½ tsp	black pepper
1	salmon steak, cut into 1-inch pieces

1	swordfish steak, cut into 1-inch pieces
1	sweet red pepper, cut into large pieces
2	medium onions, cut into large pieces
8	skewers

In a large bowl, combine lemon juice, dill, garlic, sugar, paprika, salt and pepper. Set aside 1/4 cup of marinade for basting. Marinate salmon and swordfish pieces for 15 minutes. Skewer fish, red pepper and onions. Grill, occasionally turning and basting with extra marinade, for 5 to 8 minutes, until fish is opaque and has grill marks.

Baked Red Snapper with Fennel and Green Pepper Relish

SERVES 4

*Fennel's a favourite of mine; it adds a piquant,
licorice flavour to the snapper.*

¼ cup	apple juice	1	fennel bulb, chopped (about 2 cups)
¼ cup	chopped fresh dill or ½ tsp dried	2 tbsp	lemon juice
¼ cup	chopped fresh mint or 1 tsp dried	2 tbsp	liquid honey
1	small red onion, chopped	1 tsp	black pepper
2	medium green peppers, chopped	4	6-oz red snapper fillets

In a medium mixing bowl, combine the apple juice, dill, mint, onion, green pepper, fennel, lemon juice, honey and black pepper. Mix well. Place the red snapper on a baking sheet. Spread the relish evenly on top. Bake in preheated 350°F oven for 15 to 20 minutes, or until fish is cooked through. Do not overcook.

A House of Cards

On one episode, our set wall started to cave in. I saw what was happening, but I was transfixed; I couldn't move...the wall came crashing down around me.

Oven-Baked Spicy Cod

SERVES 2 TO 4

My very spicy, oven-baked, breaded cod goes best with a cool soup (try cucumber!), a mesclun mix salad and a delicious mushroom risotto.

1 tsp	dried oregano	1 tsp	black pepper
1 tsp	onion powder	2	large cod fillets
1 tsp	garlic powder	½ cup	bread crumbs
1 tsp	cayenne pepper	¼ cup	chopped fresh parsley
1 tsp	dried basil	1 tbsp	olive oil
1 tsp	paprika	1 tsp	lemon juice
1 tsp	salt		

In a large mixing bowl, combine oregano, onion powder, garlic powder, cayenne, basil, paprika, salt and pepper. Set aside about half of this mixture; sprinkle the rest evenly over the fish. Combine the remaining spice and herb mixture with bread crumbs, parsley, olive oil, and lemon juice. Press fish in breadcrumb mixture and coat both sides. Bake in a preheated 350°F oven about 10 to 15 minutes, turning once.

The set, year 4.

Sweet Surrender

The moustache, year 4.

Apple Crisp Made Really Easy

SERVES 6

Yummy and easy. 'Nuff said.

Tip
Unless a recipe states otherwise, always preheat an oven for 10 to 15 minutes before starting to bake.

			TOPPING	
5 cups	apple slices	1 ½ cups	quick-cooking rolled oats
½ cup	lemon juice	1 cup	packed brown sugar
½ cup	apple juice	¾ cup	melted butter
1 tbsp	brown sugar	½ cup	all-purpose flour
		1 ½ tsp	ground cinnamon
		½ tsp	salt

Place apple slices on a greased 9 inch square baking dish; sprinkle with lemon juice, apple juice and brown sugar. In a medium bowl, combine oats, sugar, butter, flour, cinnamon and salt. Mix well until topping is crumbly. Sprinkle topping mixture over apples. Bake in a preheated 375°F oven for 30 to 35 minutes or until apples are soft. Serve hot, warm or cold.

Helen's Blueberry Delight

SERVES 6

*My mother—a perennial favourite on **What's for Dinner?**—is as famous for her baking as she is for playing bingo. This one's a winner!*

2 cups	graham crumbs	6 oz.	cream cheese
¾ cup	brown sugar	¾ cup	icing sugar
½ cup	butter	2 cups	blueberries
1 pkg	whipped topping mix		

Mix together graham crumbs, brown sugar, and butter; use to line a pie plate to create a crust. Prepare whipped topping as directed and fold in cream cheese and icing sugar. Fill crust with about half the cream cheese mixture. Top with blueberries followed by the remaining cream cheese mixture. Sprinkle more graham crumbs on top. Refrigerate for 1/2 hour before serving.

Variation
Replace blueberries with strawberries.

Low-Fat Option
Whipped cottage cheese or ricotta may be substituted for the cream cheese to reduce fat.

Tip
Blueberries are an excellent source of vitamin C and should be kept dry in the fridge. They will freeze for up to 6 months.

Pineapple Cake

SERVES 6

Sweet, light and delicious.

3	eggs		2 tsp	baking powder
1 cup	white sugar			Pinch salt
½ cup	vegetable oil		2 cups	sliced pineapple
2 tbsp	pineapple juice		¼ tsp	grated nutmeg
1 tsp	vanilla extract		¼ tsp	ground cinnamon
2 cups	all-purpose flour			

In a large bowl, using a beater, beat the eggs, sugar, oil, pineapple juice and vanilla for 3 minutes or until smooth. Add the flour, baking powder and salt. Beat the mixture until smooth, about 1 minute. Pour into a 9 inch x 13 inch greased pan and place the sliced pineapple on top. Sprinkle with nutmeg and cinnamon. Bake in a preheated 350°F oven for about 30 minutes or until a toothpick inserted in centre of cake comes out clean.

Kostick's Carrot and Cognac Loaf

MAKES 2 LOAVES

*The cognac makes this a most debonair carrot loaf.
If baked goods had personas, this loaf would definitely
be of the Carey Grant variety!*

1 ½ cups	vegetable oil		1 tsp	vanilla extract
2 cups	brown sugar		3 cups	all-purpose flour
2 ½ cups	finely grated carrots		1 tbsp	baking powder
2 cups	mixed candied fruit		2 tsp	baking soda
1 ½ to 2 cups	raisins		2 tsp	cinnamon
1 cup	chopped walnuts		1 tsp	salt
4	eggs		½ tsp	ground cloves
2 tbsp	cognac		¼ tsp	nutmeg

Pour oil into a large bowl; gradually blend in sugar. Mix in carrots, candied fruit, raisins, walnuts, eggs, cognac and vanilla. In a separate bowl, sift together flour, baking powder, baking soda, cinnamon, salt, cloves and nutmeg. Mix flour and carrot mixtures together well. Pour into a well-greased 6 inch x 10 inch loaf pan. Bake in a preheated 350°F oven for 1 hour or until a toothpick inserted in the centre comes our clean.

"Okay, that's it! Never again." "Yeah, right, I could only be so lucky."

Kenny's Peanut Butter Cookies

MAKES 3 DOZEN COOKIES

The cinnamon gives these peanutty treats a certain
"je ne sais quois"...

1 cup	butter	2	eggs
1 cup	smooth peanut butter	2 tsp	vanilla
1 cup	white sugar	3 cups	all-purpose flour
1 cup	brown sugar	2 tsp	baking soda
1/4 tsp	ground cinnamon		

In a large bowl, cream together butter, peanut butter, white sugar, brown sugar and cinnamon; add eggs and mix until smooth. Stir in vanilla. Add flour and soda; mix well. Roll batter into small balls, place on greased cookie sheet. Press gently with a fork. Bake in a preheated 375°F oven for 12 to 15 minutes or until cookies are lightly browned.

Poor Ken!

Our director, Dennis Saunders, would come out on set prior to taping to give us instructions on what he wanted us to do. Since I'm not good at focussing too long on what anyone has to say (attention deficit disorder?), whenever he walked away I'd turn to Mary Jo and ask, "Is there anything I need to know?" Her response was always, "Definitely not."

Chocolate Chip Coconut Cookies

MAKES ABOUT 3 DOZEN COOKIES

*This is my season-four favourite: largely because there are
only 58 calories, and 3 grams of fat, in each of these cookies.*

8	egg whites		3 cups	sweetened coconut
½ cup	sugar		½ cup	chocolate chips
½ cup	all-purpose flour		1 tsp	vanilla extract

In a glass bowl, beat egg whites until stiff. Fold in sugar and flour. Add coconut, chocolate chips and vanilla, and mix well. Drop batter by tablespoonfuls onto greased cookie sheets. Bake in a preheated 325°F oven for 10 to 15 minutes or until edges are lightly browned.

Taking It Off

The very last episode of year five was a show-stopping striptease. Actually, it was our tribute to exotic dancers. On camera, to a raunchy number, Mr. Kostick took it off. But boxer shorts and black socks is definitely not a good look for Mr. Kostick. (This man should always keep his clothes on!)

Orange Oatmeal Cookies

MAKES ABOUT 3 DOZEN COOKIES

My Mom makes these for my neighbour Gill,
who loves to dip them in tea.

1 cup	all-purpose flour		1	egg, unbeaten
1 cup	white sugar		2 tbsp	grated orange rind
2 tsp	baking powder		2 tbsp	orange juice concentrate
½ tsp	salt		1 ½ cups	quick-cooking rolled oats
½ tsp	ground nutmeg		1 cup	coconut
½ cup	shortening			

Grease cookie sheets and preheat oven to 375°F. Sift flour, sugar, baking powder, salt and nutmeg together into a medium bowl. Add shortening, egg, orange rind and orange juice concentrate. Beat until smooth and well-blended. Mix in the oats and coconut. Drop dough by teaspoonfuls, about 3 inches apart, onto a greased cookie sheet. Bake until edges are lightly browned, approximately 12 to 15 minutes.

Cinnamon Granola Cookies

MAKES 2 TO 3 DOZEN COOKIES

Here's a great tasting cookie you can feel good about eating!

½ cup	unsalted butter	½ tsp	baking soda
½ cup	honey	1 cup	raisins
4 tbsp	brown sugar	¼ cup	dried apricots
1 tsp	cinnamon	¼ cup	dates
1 cup	all-purpose flour	¼ cup	chopped nuts
¼ cup	quick-cooking rolled oats	1 tsp	vanilla extract

In a large bowl, cream together butter, honey, sugar and cinnamon. Add flour, oats and soda; mix well. Mix in raisins, apricots, dates, nuts and vanilla. Drop by teaspoonfuls onto greased cookie sheets. Bake in a preheated 375°F oven about 8 to 10 minutes.

Heh, heh, heh, this is so much fun...is that gun loaded?

The Easiest Shortbread

MAKES ABOUT 2 DOZEN COOKIES

*This may very well be the easiest shortbread recipe
you ever make.*

1 cup	butter	1 ½ cups	flour
¼ tsp	vanilla	¼ cup	red and green cherries
½ cup	icing sugar		

In a large bowl, cream butter and vanilla until smooth. Add icing sugar and beat well. Add flour and combine. Form balls, place on an ungreased sheet and depress the centres with your finger. Place red and green cherries in centres of the cookies. Bake in preheated 375°F oven for about 10 minutes or until edges turn slightly brown. Transfer onto paper towels to cool.

Variation
Try adding candied peel and/or slivered almonds to the mixture before baking.

Trigger happy.

Grandpa's Bran Muffins

MAKES 18 LARGE MUFFINS

*Helen's Grandpa's muffins are so much better
than store-bought ones!*

2 ½ cups	all-bran cereal		½ tsp	vanilla
1 ½ cups	milk		1 ½ cups	flour
1 cup	honey		1 cup	raisins or chopped dates
½ cup	warm water		1 ¼ tsp	baking soda
½ cup	vegetable oil			Pinch salt
2	eggs			

Place all-bran in a bowl and add milk, honey, warm water, oil, eggs and vanilla. Stir with wooden spoon. Add flour, raisins or dates, soda and salt; mix just enough to combine. Bake in a preheated 350°F oven 30 to 35 minutes or until brown.

Variation
Add chopped nuts
with the raisins or
dates.

Tip
Eating high-fibre bread
or cereal products like
bran muffins is a smart
alternative to higher
fat snacks.

Index

maple syrup, 52, 55, 72, 129

mint, 74, 130, 153, 203, 209
  lemon grilled pork chops with, 179
  relish, red pepper, honey and, 30
  scallop, fennel and, salad, 18
  seared spring lamb with, 189
  and strawberry salad dressing, 28
  tofu stir-fry with orange and, 117

mushrooms, 31, 32, 80, 82, 87, 99, 106, 116, 121, 149, 150, 199
  button, 45, 67, 76, 83, 88, 122, 125, 164, 170, 204
  corn and red pepper with, 67
  fettuccine with chicken and, 95
  grilled beef tenderloin with, 170
  grilled portobello, 124
  grilled portobello over penne, 101
  portobello, 11, 88, 101, 124
  risotto, 88
  shiitake, 88
  and vegetable kabobs, 122
  zucchini stuffed with, 125

mussels
  seafood spaghetti, 96
  in white wine, 199
  mustard dijon, 33, 146, 204

N

noodles
  egg, 109
  grilled shrimp over, 109
  oriental-style, with bacon, 108
  spicy, with tofu, 116
  stir-fried, and vegetables with curry, 126

nuts
  almond, 12
  cashews, 81
  pine, 32

O

oatmeal cookies, orange, 218

olives, 188
  black, 161, 182
  green, 187
  pork stew with red wine and, 182

onion
  calf's liver and, 173
  cooking, 44, 45, 51, 52, 53, 55, 56, 59, 68, 69, 76, 80, 81, 83, 84, 87, 88, 89, 90, 94, 97, 99, 100, 107, 108, 112, 125, 134, 144, 147, 149, 159, 171, 181, 183, 187, 188
  purple, 121
  red, 14, 18, 20, 30, 42, 63, 74, 95, 102, 121, 122, 127, 128, 133, 138, 142, 147, 153, 163, 164, 165, 168, 170, 172, 173, 175, 182, 185, 192
  white, 47, 48

orange, 14
  chicken, grilled, 137
  fruit salad, 13
  juice, 6, 12, 14, 40, 62, 137, 161, 169, 178, 196
  low-fat coleslaw with almonds and, 12
  mandarin, 117, 166
  mandarin, beef, 166

oatmeal cookies, 218
  sauce, 206
  tofu stir-fry with mint and, 117

oregano, 122

P

paella
  stove-top, 85, 86
  vegetarian, 87

papaya, 168

paprika, 202

parsley, 5, 12, 14, 21, 34, 40, 46, 57, 59, 65, 66, 76, 80, 83, 91, 94, 96, 97, 99, 100, 104, 112, 117, 122, 127, 130, 131, 136, 140, 141, 146, 153, 155, 159, 171, 178, 179, 180, 185, 186, 188, 192, 194, 198, 199, 200, 210
  Italian, 109, 204
  lemon, vinaigrette, 27

pasta
  bow tie, 97, 113
  fettuccine, 95, 198
  fusilli, 14, 104, 106, 107
  linguini, 110
  macaroni, 94
  noodles, 108, 109, 116, 126

penne, 15, 100, 101, 102, 103
  primavera, 107
  rigatoni, 111
  rotini, 98
  salmon, 113
  shell, 112
  spaghetti, 96, 99, 126
  Spanish-style Mediterranean, 112

peanut butter, 116
  cookies, 216

pears
  fruit salad, 13
  sauteéd, 74

peas, 56, 81, 126, 129, 144, 187
  snow, 126

penne
  with beef tenderloin and fresh basil, 102
  with blue cheese and spinach, 100
  grilled portobello mushrooms over, 101
  salad with feta, 15
  with turkey sausage and sweet red